LISTEN UP!

THE OTHER SIDE
IS
TALKING

KELLE SUTLIFF

Also by Kelle Sutliff:

Pearls of Wisdom :
30 Inspirational Ideas
to Live Your Best Life Now!

Copyright January 2014 by Kelle Sutliff

<u>Credits</u>

Edited by: Joan Schaublin

Typesetting/design/layout: Robert Jacoby of The Master Key Press

Inquiries should be addressed to:

Kelle Sutliff, 505 Middlesex Turnpike, Suite 13, Billerica MA 01821

ISBN: 978-0-9915068-0-4   Print
            978-0-9915068-1-1   Digital
E-mail: psychichmedium@verizon.net

Website: www.psychicmediumkelle.com

Published by: Tri Circle Publishing

Contact the above address to order, or call/fax/e-mail for more information about this book.

Dedication

This book is dedicated to my beautiful children

Matthew, Avery, and Haley.

Thank you for picking me as your Mom.

I love you so very much.

Remember to always follow your intuition.

It will always be there to serve and protect you

throughout your life.

Remember you cannot hold bliss in your fist.

You can hold bliss only in your open hand

–Osho-

ACKNOWLEDGEMENTS

I have been so fortunate to "grow up medium." Every single day, I thank God for the gift I have been given. It's pretty rewarding the work I do because it is so spiritual to me. There was much encouragement along the four year path of writing this book. I was given significant support by family, friends, clients, and most of all, my children.

Matthew, Avery, and Haley were my permanent cheerleaders, asking me "When is your book going to be done? How many pages did you write today?" and my favorite, "You mean it's not done yet?" Well, it's done now kids, and I hope you like it.

There are several people I would like to mention: My husband Tom, for all of your technical help and support on this project. Thanks for letting me be the point and click girl that I am. My dear family: My mother Marilyn, my sisters and brothers - Carey, Denise, Pat, Ritchie, Bob, and Jeff, for trusting in my gift as a psychic medium and understanding that "she really isn't crazy." They have certainly given me the encouragement when I needed it. I can't forget my father Ritchie, for he is in Spirit. Trust me when I say that he gave me loads of signs while preparing for this journey.

I know he'll be vigorously promoting this book on the other side. I can hear him now: "My daughter Kelle just wrote a book! It's really great! It talks about us and where we are. Have your friends and family buy a copy!" I also know he'll be rounding up the forces to make *Listen Up! The Other Side IS Talking* a success, being the salesman that he was.

My dad would often tell me in a private message "Hey Kel, you're looking good!" This was a joke that started between us when I was eleven, on a vacation in Myrtle Beach, South Carolina. With every accomplishment thereafter, whether it be my high school graduation, my college graduation, or my wedding day, I would hear "Hey Kel, how ya lookin'?" "Lookin' good Dad, lookin' good!" I would reply, and then he would say again,

"Your lookin' good, Kel" with that twinkle in his eye! This book is a "lookin' good" moment for the two of us. His inspiration is present in many stories throughout this book, but the best story he gave me was the wonderful relationship we shared. I'm so blessed to be able to say that. I would also like to thank my teachers and my psychic friends, Linda Lawrence, Bridget Benson, Robbie Holtz, Mark Anthony, Glyn Edwards, John Holland, Renee Baribeau, Nancy Smith, Peggy Querze, Rosie Hanlon, Mary Lee Trettenero, and Richard Lanza, for helping me know our network really is normal. Being psychic is just who we are, right everybody?

I can't forget to acknowledge my past and present radio stations for letting me have a home for my show *Psychic Cup of Coffee*. Many thanks to *CBS Radio*'s Brandon Jaksim and Lisa Rodman, for their wonderful dedication to my program. *Psychic Cup of Coffee* is still keeping intuition "real" on *Transformational Talk Radio*, so everyone can understand how this whole psychic gig works! I am honored to have a radio voice on this network.

I've been blessed with friends all over the world. I'm a millionaire twenty times over in the friends department. How lucky am I? You know who you are. I'd need another book to list all of you. I want to say thank you for all your love, and all the laughs throughout my life. This book could not have been written without those beautiful friend outlets.

One friend in particular, who was a big catalyst for this book by keeping me on target, is Linda Brown, who's been my secretary throughout this whole project. Thank you, thank you; you have been a gift to me in so many ways.

Many thanks to my editor Joan Schaublin, who helped me to fine-tune my manuscript and make it the beautiful book it is today. Your spiritual nature showed up in every period, comma, or new suggestion that you gave to me. I know our connection will continue to be rewarded many times over.

Rob Jacoby of The Master Key Press, and author of *The Map To Love: How To Navigate The Art Of The Heart*, brought his expertise to the table and is truly the master of layout. His creativity helped make this book flow and the pages pop! Thank you, Rob, for your wonderful design work on this book.

Lastly, to all in spirit who I've connected with and to all of the missing I've found, it's been my pleasure and I'm honored to have worked with you.

Big hugs all around,
Kelle

Contents

Contents

FORWARD

I am a great believer in fate, especially in the work that I do as a clairvoyant medium. I first spoke to Kelle when my book, *When Tomorrow Speaks to Me: Memoirs of an Irish Medium*, was published in 2010. From the very first moment we met, there was a connection between us. Kelle radiates warmth and sincerity in her work as a clairvoyant medium. She has the gift of being able to reach out to people and bring them comfort and the reassurance that their loved ones are still able to communicate with them. She also conveys the real and soothing knowledge that they understand the pain and loss that those of us left behind are going through.

In this book, she shares her experiences in an honest and straightforward manner. You will better understand how we do the work we do as mediums, and how you, the reader, can also benefit from "waking up" to your own abilities. She encourages us to learn to recognize the signs and symbols that are always around us, and guides us in how to use them to our benefit in our daily lives.

We all have a God given ability to listen to our intuition and stay connected to those we think we have lost, and with humor and grace, Kelle walks us through the process of learning to trust our inner knowing.

You will also have an opportunity to renew your relationship with the Earth, and all the hidden wonders it is begging us to remember. Kelle helps us to see that the planet itself is talking to us, if we will only quiet our inner chatter and listen. She assures us that collectively, we can make a difference before it's too late. This is good news for all of us.

My hope is that one day Kelle and I will work together in order to help people blend the material world and the eternal world into the seamless, one dimension we understand it to be. I have no doubt that this book will give you the tools and the desire to join us.

Love, Light & Happiness Always
Bridget Benson

INTRODUCTION

We all come into this world with a mission, and some of the things we get assigned to do are pre-planned for us. They are the life experiences that we never anticipated having when we were eight years old and someone asked, "What do you want to be when you grow up?" When I was eight I wanted to be a teacher. I can remember playing school a lot back then. Since I went to Catholic School, I was always the nun teaching! Little did I know that I would grow up to be a teacher, but of a very different kind; one that truly guides others. I am a psychic medium. I am a conduit for the souls on the other side. I look at the work I do as a spiritual journey. With twelve years of Catholic education, everything has to have a spiritual meaning, or else!

For whatever reason, I was given the ability to do this work. I absolutely love to share it, promote it, and feel it. Every time I read for someone, I feel like I am talking to my best friend. It's me and you and all of your guides, communicating and directing information through our love vibrations, centering our souls and becoming one with Spirit. It's that connection that enables me to give the information. My clients are meant to feel it and to capture the vibration that will help them feel whole again. Life leads us down some crazy paths, doesn't it? We are constantly redirecting ourselves. How we handle those redirections are key. It's when those curveballs are thrown at us that we need to remember; we can get reassurance from our passed loved ones and guides, to assist us day by day. It's their new role to help us, and they want to! As a medium, I'm telling you that you can consult with me for the connection to get messages from a passed loved one, but that you don't have to. You have the tools to work with your own intuition and to listen to your own "inner yearning of learning."

How often do we tune ourselves out? If we were all cell phones and our inner knowing was calling, I wonder if we would even answer! When our cell phones ring in our current lives, no matter where we are, we answer! You need to know right now that your inner voice *is* ringing. Do not send it to spiritual voicemail. Your spiritual voicemail is FULL and you need to delete the messages that don't serve you; the messages you've stored full of self-doubt or abuse; the ones that tell you that you're never good enough. We're all on overload, and it's time to strip away the unnecessary tasks that we've assigned ourselves and that we think are so important. They're really not. It's pretty pathetic how we act sometimes, isn't it?

We think we have to be the perfect Mom or Dad. We think we have to be the best at everything! "Best, Best Overload" has taken over our lives and we don't want to deal with it anymore. Our kids are feeling the pressure too. We get so caught up in all that stuff that we forget why we're here. It's time to take care of you and your intuitive needs, and to learn how to pamper your psychic self along the way. Just keeping it simple and not over complicating your thoughts can do wonders for your soul.

Did you know that your brain thinks about 70,000 thoughts a day? Is there kindness in the thoughts that you're feeding to your brain and soul? It's time to make a shift in your thought processes and I'm here to help you. It's time to start listening to you and only you. You have an important obligation to yourself. Please don't throw your inner knowing into your spiritual voicemail. The time has come for you to listen and to take action. It'll make you feel good and whole again, I promise.

Remember, we are born perfect. It's a shame we don't continue to live our lives as our already perfected selves. Instead, we try to make better what's already divine, and end up screwing things up and neglecting ourselves. In the book *21 Steps to Reach Your Spirit*, Santoshan says "Our true nature is forever trying to tell us how we should be." In my world, these are pretty important words to live by. All we have to do is listen to our very own built in perfection, which our intuition gives to us every day.

It's important that you prioritize your good ole' self. I say the word "self" because there is no one else and no one better. It's just you. Self really does matter, especially today. Our current environment is changing. We need to redefine ourselves every day by telling ourselves we're good people, we're deserving of good, and we're deserving of a good world to live in.

If we don't take our quiet time to define "our goods" who will, and what will happen to our energy level? It can do one of two things. Either our energy level will drop very low putting us in a tired, rundown state, or the energy around us will become so frenzied that we can't cope with it. We'll become hyper, hysterical, or worse yet, explosive, only to bring ourselves down again. Have you noticed any of these traits in yourself lately? Why do we feel so emotional and pissed off when we shouldn't be? Why are all the details of our lives that should be going right, all of a sudden going wrong?

Why is this happening?

It's happening because our energy and personal light has changed. And it will continue to change. That's the good news! You've shifted. We're all way overdue for greater development and enlightenment. So where do you fit in? Are you the low, low, lows or the high, high, highs? Where is the happy medium in you, the balance you're craving? What gives with all this change and information that you're seeking?

It's there to show you that the most important change is that which creates the perfect equilibrium for your soul.

Our physical body needs balance for all of our organs to work. Doesn't it make sense that our soul needs balance for it to work as well? The soul has many layers of function. And just as important as preserving our good health by showing up for our yearly physical, our soul needs "check-ups" too. The time is now to achieve this plateau of balance, but we need to listen to our intuition, our guides, and our loved ones that have passed on for signs and direction. We need to be quiet and calm in order to be guided. We can't do this and expect a positive effect if we let our lives fill up with chaos.

In order for you to prevent the chaos from coming your way, you have to ground and protect your space ahead of time. Otherwise, the chaos will find you. Chaos has a great memory and never forgets where it went last. It can always find a victim and there are too many people inviting it into their lives. I ground myself at least three times a day. I call it the "breakfast, lunch, and dinner plan." It can be as simple as saying out loud, "I am grounded for the highest and best good today!" I wrote a whole chapter, called *Daily Cup of Calm*, to this very practice. If you'd like to read it, you can find it in *Pearls of Wisdom - 30 Inspirational Ideas to Live Your Best Life Now*! with NY Times best-selling authors like Jack Canfield, Marci Shimoff, Janet Bray Attwood and Chris Attwood, as well as other bright stars of transformational leadership.

In this book I will help you learn to trust your intuition and to understand how all this psychic stuff works. I promise you that the person you are after you read this will be different than the person you were before. You will be a better you, your *true* self, and much better prepared for the changing environment that lay ahead. And Boy, Oh Boy, is it ever changing! Let me show you how you can create a better game plan for yourself while dealing with all of this great change. I will teach you how to listen to your soul. I have a beautiful sign in my house that reads *"Make time for the quiet moments as God whispers and the world is loud"* It's so important to turn our inner dialogue OFF and to be peaceful so our intuition can guide us as it did when we were newly born and perfect. It's time to regain trust in your insight and to let it flow through you. Your intuitive gift, that layer of your soul, is waiting to work with you.

After reading this book, my hope is that you'll have a better understanding of how you and your psychic insight work, and how the signs and symbols from your loved ones are energy being used to give us messages. If we'd only pay attention and pause to listen, we'd realize our loved ones have been "dialing in" with their own form of texting for years. Everyone needs to understand how it all works, press their own soul's refresh button, and gain back trust in their insights.

This book can be used as a guide, and will give you tons of examples of how spirit works and influences us every day. It's true. The other side is talking. Your psychic closet is about to be opened. Prepare to regain your soul's balance and have all these soul layers revealed to you. Are you ready?

Ok.

Let's Go.

-Kelle

THE
BEGINNING

When people ask me "When did you become a psychic?" I answer "Technically, my whole life." When asked "When did you know you were different?" I always answer "It's my normal, isn't it yours?" I always thought everyone had this psychic gift. At nine years old I remember my Grandma Sloan dying of cancer. It was soon after that she was visiting me at night. I'd wake up in the morning and tell my mom "Grandma Sloan was in my room last night." I'd describe what her clothes looked like. I'd recount the conversation I'd had with her, sharing every detail. My mom would say "Oh, really?" and continue with her morning rituals, as mothers tend to do. These experiences would come often, and so would another "Oh, really?" from my mother. It wasn't frightening. It was just a matter of fact, a part of me.

My grandmother was a believer in the psychic. She was a farmer from Illinois, and a very intuitive person. She planted many a crop by the phase of the moon, making sure everything was lined up just right. It's true that psychic abilities run in families, so why wouldn't my grandmother come through to her clairvoyant granddaughter, me, the child who hadn't blocked her psychic ability? I gave her messages to my mom, being as open as I was at the ripe old age of nine, but not really understanding the work I was doing. I was the conduit giving messages from souls on the other side. It was my normal as a little girl, and the secret was, I thought everyone else did it too. I would soon learn that my normal was definitely not everyone's normal.

Now think about how this whole message thing works, and question. Why *wouldn't* it work this way? You share a lifetime with your loved one and all the energy that's created between the two of you merges. Do you think it just dissipates when one of you leaves this earth? No, it continues; it constantly flows, merging with your energy. Why do you think you have memories of this person? It's because of the constant flow of energy that continues to make its way through your energetic fields whenever your loved one wants to come through to you. He/She uses the energy that was created by the two of you. This is how it happens. It's from that love vibration, the link through which messages are given and received, that we are shown, once again, that we are still connected.

As a child, I thought everyone had dreams populated by people they didn't know. I thought that was normal. I never had people I knew here on Earth in my dreams. When I dreamt, it was always of lots of unknown people. What I realized, after accepting "my job" as a medium in my mid-thirties, was that those people were actually souls who had crossed over. I never had a fear of my gift as a kid. I was just afraid of the usual kid stuff, like what might be hiding in the basement, or of the "gators" that were always under the bed. I never felt any fear of my friends from the other side. They were comfortable and safe for me, but never, ever frightening.

I'm sure that most people who have had a loved one die have also had them come back in dreams. Why is that? Because when we're sleeping is when we are the most psychic. Our bodies and minds are relaxed enough that we can receive messages from our loved ones. Most people will say, "Oh that was just a dream!" But the deeper reality is, it wasn't just a dream, and it's time for everyone to listen up. More of us are experiencing connections with our loved ones that have passed on. Why? The simple answer is because we can. We need to wake up and realize the power of who they are. We need to use our intuition and listen to the messages given to us. During the coming years our intuition will really be changing, just as our Earth and societies are changing. Doesn't it make sense that the other side would be changing too? As the other side's energetic field lifts to another dimension, ours will be rising to meet it. The messages that will be coming through to each one of us will be amazing, and the best part is we'll all have the higher consciousness to have access to them.

Our intuition is to be used to become more open-minded and to help us to leave our narrow-mindedness behind. As our community vibration rises, we'll all get that link and connection needed to receive messages from our loved ones. Get ready to practice what you are meant to preach and be the best little intuitive you can be. Change is coming, ready or not! It will come easiest for those of us willing to trust our intuition, and thankfully, most of society will. The abundance of inner knowing that will be given to you will feel so familiar that it'll be like a long lost best friend showing up for a visit. The dead will always reassure their loved ones that they're okay. They want to comfort family and friends. As souls, that's part of their job now; to help enlighten the people left behind. Souls have this job to do, so let them work for you. Allow their messages to be heard.

If we really paid attention to the daily coincidences in our lives and realized that they're not coincidences at all, we'd "hear" them as the messages they are meant to be. For instance, let's say you're thinking about your friend, and just then the phone rings. You pick it up and say, "Hi! I was just thinking about you!" Coincidence? I personally don't think so. When that happens to me, I say to my friends, "So you got my message and you're returning the call!" If you pay attention you'll see this happen more and more. You think of someone and you bump into them at the mall; you're driving along and you suddenly decide to take another route just for the heck of it, and it turns out there was a major accident on the route you normally take. As insignificant as these examples may seem, I could go on and on with more and I'm sure you could too. These "coincidences" are not mere accidents. They're signs being given to you by your guides and intuition. It's your own inner wisdom that's "blabbing" to you and you need to listen to it. If we took a smidgen of our inner knowing and used it daily, my oh my, would our lives ever change. How do we best listen to our inner guides, and how can we practice? When you get a "hunch" (if you want to call it that) or "direction" (as I prefer to call it), do you blow it off and tell yourself that you were just being smart by taking a different route to work, or do you acknowledge that little whisper of knowing that told you "Don't go down that highway"?

We need to just accept our "hunches" and trust them for what they are. Have faith in the guides that interact with you and know that it's quite okay. That's what they're here for; to enlighten your life choices. You have a whole team around you to work with your intuition. They can be passed loved ones, angels, or guides, all aspects of the higher realm of living that come to work with you. All you have to do is ask and *trust*. Did you notice I said the word "living" when I talked about angels, guides, and loved ones? That's because I do believe they live. Sure, they've switched from this life on Earth as they knew it to another, but they continue to live in life and the circle of soul consciousness. I would have a hard time trusting advice coming from a dead angel, wouldn't you? "Calling all dead angels! I need some help!" It doesn't sit well does it? So think of this energy realm as life, living and healthy, and then you can understand it all from a positive perspective. It's all there to help you embrace their work and they will be right there to aid you.

As a child I understood this really, really easily. Then I had to grow up and all that changed. I had to deal with what society thought of me as a psychic medium. It hurt the ego a bit, but it made me sympathetic to how untrusting people can be of themselves. They look at death as this black and white affair. I'm telling them it's quite different. I know because I feel it every time I read for someone. Death is just another facet of life, and it's quite colorful!

When was the last time you sat in a chair and were quiet? I mean, really quiet; no mind running, no "To Do" list bouncing around in your head, no phone to answer. I call this quiet time "the personal time out chair," but this time out chair isn't about punishment. It's a time out for you to connect with your guides and to get to know your inner voice. You're not using this time to think, but to receive. It's the hardest thing to learn but once you have, it's like a magic balm for you and your soul. It's about finding that balance of ease and stillness that helps you grow intuitively.

When I sit, which I do a couple of times a day, it's because I need to in order to stay grounded and clear for the readings I do every day. If you're not a medium, you don't have to sit three times a day, but you should do it at least once a day. If you do, I promise that you'll learn a lot about yourself. You may even decide to go ahead and do it two or three times a day, just because it feels good and makes such a positive difference in your life.

So what do you do? First, find a comfy chair and sit with your feet planted firmly on the ground. This posture will help you stay grounded. Next, say a prayer. It can be any prayer that you feel helps connect you with spirit. As you connect, ask for guidance, and let all the gook that clutters your mind drain away.

As you quiet your mind and welcome the stillness, ask your questions. It's what you hear and feel that will confirm your answers. Hear those whispers of thought and just let them flow through you, without attachment. Breathe in and then breathe out; inhale, exhale; that's right. Remember, breathing properly is cleansing, so don't forget to breathe. As newborns, we breathed perfectly. As we age, we forget to take these cleansing breaths. "Breathe out the old and breathe in the new" is what I like to say to myself. What do you think happens when you do this? You release the unhealthy energy and a new, refreshing, and stimulating breath takes its place. Those newborns have it down pat, don't they? We need to relax and replenish ourselves like just like a newborn does. This new energy calms and feeds your senses and refreshes your body. Take a moment now, as you read this, to breathe in deeply and then breathe out fully. Aaaah... Doesn't that feel better?

As funny as it is to say that we need to breathe with our body, we really do need to remember to take deep, cleansing breaths daily. Did you just take a deep breath? Why? Because your body knows what it needs. Our physical bodies need to feel calm, so our mental bodies can too. We'll become centered and whole within our spiritual body, and get whispers of insight when we ask for them, and yes, when we need them most.

It's Kind of Like the 1-2 Punch

By doing simple breathing exercises we can start breathing correctly. This will always give us the same, perfect result; a calm, relaxed state of being. It's in this relaxed, calm, and quiet place that we learn to connect with spirit.

Are you ready to connect? Can you imagine the dose of calm that will fill your body if you do this simple little exercise of breathing consciously as you start your day? This is one grace that we can easily give our body and it will be grateful.

Your spirit, your soul, needs grace. Yes, grace. "By the grace of God" - we use that term a lot. It *is* by the grace of God that we are given the gift to connect to spirit. It's the universal gift of choice. It's a choice to listen to our inner selves, to share our inner gifts with others, and to listen to what's most important within us. When we are willing to accept grace, we will receive it. We then need to acknowledge it and protect it. Relish what you've been given by listening to your intuition; that small, inner voice that we so often blow off and decide not to take seriously. See what happens...

I was a medium. I just didn't know it. After I married and decided to have a family, here came my psychic self, ready to take on the world and get busy! After all, everything else happening was new; a marriage, new homes, and children. Why shouldn't I have a new career? Because, as I soon realized, I wasn't ready. I stopped it. Yes, you can control psychic ability. You can decide when it's the right time to use it, and only let it in only when you're ready.

My biggest problem is that when people know I'm psychic, I have to be extra careful to set boundaries to keep from experiencing the negative side of things. This can easily happen when you're a medium. Always "being on" and not creating boundaries can have you tapping into energy that you don't want to tap into. That's why it's important to find someone to guide you as you start exploring your own abilities. It's important to use your psychic self for the proper purpose. Don't allow it to be used by some foreign form of energy that's not healthy for you. It's the "good door - bad door" policy; always work with the good door! Because I didn't want anything to interfere with having my children, I put a big stop sign on it. I just wasn't willing to take the chance of opening up any bad doors into my life.

I had three kids in three years, and my girls were Irish twins; only eleven months apart! Yes, I had a busy household. I thought I was so wise that right out loud, while making baby formula in my kitchen one morning, I yelled "I'm ready to be psychic and use my gift!" As soon as the words flew out of my mouth, all kinds of metaphysical activity started. I realized in that moment that I had no idea what I was doing. Holy crap! What had I done?

My children were babies. Matthew was three, Avery was thirteen months, and newborn Haley, was two months. My house was nuts. Oh yeah, and a husband who seemed to always be switching jobs and getting promoted every time I had a baby. His work also involved lots of travel. As if all this wasn't enough, my "Third Eye" had opened. And I had *asked* for it! Your third eye is your intuition and psychic ability. On your physical body, it's located between your eyebrows on your forehead. It's also one of your chakra points.

At home I would see energy flashing everywhere. At night I was feeding two babies. I would feed Haley every three hours, and toss Avery a bottle whenever she woke up during the night. Meanwhile, I'm connecting with people who had crossed over, just like I had when I was a kid. My guides were probably thrilled. I could hear them shouting "She's back! She's back!" Now remember, I had been intuitive all of my life, but I had pressed pause for a lot of years before I allowed *IT* to show itself to me again. So technically, I'm a late bloomer! (Not really, but that's my story and I'm sticking to it!) I kinda blew off spirit for about twenty years, but my guides all knew I would come around. Today this girl is here to stay!

I was the new beam of light in Braintree, Massachusetts and the party was at my house, with all of my babies in tow! Boy was I tired! People would say, "Kel, you look so worn out." Well no kidding! They were assuming it was because of "new mother syndrome" with its predictable lack of sleep. If they only knew how busy life really was for me! My bedroom had never been so active! All I was doing was feeding babies and sending people into the light all night long, and I *really* didn't know what the hell I was doing.

One night during my early morning ritual, which always took place between 1:00 am and 3:00 am, (this is the time of day when the veil is thinnest, allowing psychic energy to get through to us) I was crossing a child over. He had auburn colored hair and was wearing blue pajamas. I would guess he was around seven or eight years old. This child could see the Christ light ready to carry him over to the other side, but he wouldn't go. His back was to me and I kept coaxing him, telling him to "Go into the light". He still just would not go. Now, I had never had a problem crossing anyone over before, especially a child. I said "You need to go into the light. It's ok, trust me." He then turned around and I could see that the whole side of his face and body had been burned. This poor child had died in a fire and was too afraid of the light to cross into it. I was stunned! I kept encouraging him and telling him he was loved and safe, that nothing would burn him or harm him. I kept repeating that he was safe, that it was where he needed to go, and that he was healed. Then all of a sudden, off he went.

I woke up from this in a state of panic and with tears streaming down my face. I decided right then and there that I needed someone to help me with this transition stuff, because I had no idea what I was doing. (I really *did* know, but wouldn't find that out until later.) As a child, I had done it easily. At that time it was just my normal. As an adult, it was scaring the hell out of me! Now it seemed that I needed permission and guidance to do this work, when as a child I just did it without thinking. Remember, it was a natural part of my world back then, absent of fear. Luckily for me, there was a metaphysical store in my town called *Open Doors*.

I mustered up the courage to make my very professional phone call to them, with a baby crying in the background and while hiding in the closet so I could talk without my other two finding me. If you have kids, you're familiar with not having a moment to yourself.

Richard Lanza, the psychic owner of the store, told me about the class he was offering called *Intuitive Mastery*. It was a year of intense study of all kinds of psychic and healing modalities. We would study Reiki, Therapeutic Touch, ESP, Dowsing, Psychic Development, and Mediumship. "What's that?" I wondered. "Who cares?" It sounded exciting! I quickly said "Sign me up!" As if my life wasn't already impossible enough! A three year old, a fourteen month old, and a three month old, a husband who was traveling two weeks out of the month, and my family out of state! It doesn't get much worse than that in the "give me some help!" department. I was going to take these weekly workshops for a year? Well, apparently so, because I did it. I don't know how I did it, but by the "Grace of God" I did it. Grace is very good when she needs to be, and with my guides pushing me, I managed it and I completed it. Trust me; there were days when I could hardly wait to get out the door to revel in some of my new found freedom.

I had found my new self... my *real* self. I didn't know I was a medium until I took this course. I didn't even know what a medium was, but it all became clear to me. It explained the experiences I had growing up, the people I didn't know in my dreams, my predictions, and how I knew when babies were going to be born and when people were getting ready to die. The twenty years that I thought I had shut out my abilities, really wasn't a shutdown at all. I had been having psychic experiences all along; I just hadn't been accepting them. I had let the psychic ego take over and hadn't trusted my true voice.

I really thought my calling was to do healing work like therapeutic touch, and I do currently practice therapeutic touch. I work with adults and children going through cancer. But my real calling was to use all this work to help me evolve into the psychic medium I am today. Everything that I thought I never wanted to be during my twenty year shut down, I am today.

In one of the Intuitive Mastery classes, we had to do a weekend called "Who Am I?" All weekend (no kidding!) we asked this one question again and again, and answered everyone in our class. Who am I? Mother, daughter, wife, teacher, etc... and the list went on and on. You tend to learn a lot about yourself when the only question you can ask in a weekend is "Who Am I?" You process your life and how you feel about the roles you play and why you're really here. I hated that question by Sunday night of that weekend. The good news is I finally knew who I really was - a psychic medium. Yahoo! I had accepted myself! I knew my guides were cheering for me! It all made sense to me now, but what would I do with it? Fortunately, Richard Lanza would bring in great teachers to study and learn from.

I studied with Nancy Garber, a famous medium in Boston, for two years. I learned from John Holland of New Hampshire and Brenda Lawrence, Glynn Edwards, and Gordon Smith, all from England. I would take courses by any medium I could find.

I did everything I could to understand what I was about, and to practice connecting to Spirit. I was able to read, and Richard got me exposure on a radio show. There I was, a newbie, and now I'm on the radio and nailing it! I quickly learned that the most important aspect of this work was learning to trust myself to be a conduit to the other side. You're always afraid when you first start out that you'll say the wrong thing. Trust is the hardest part of mediumship to learn. When you can feel, sense, and hear the information coming from Spirit, then you can accept your ability as being right and true. I was becoming the Spirit messenger I was meant to be. I had found myself, and guess what? This is who I am.

So now let's fast forward this journey about twelve years. Now I'm a medium reading for thousands of people. I'm a psychic detective. I'm a radio show host and I teach psychic development classes in the Boston area. My teacher gig that I had always wanted really did happen, and I didn't even have to wear a black habit to educate my students! Back in the day, when we Catholic kids would play school, we'd get a towel to put around our head to make a habit. This would complete the teacher/nun package. It's all in how you were brought up and what you were exposed to, isn't it? Sister Patty Ann would be very proud!

When I work now I actually rarely wear black, but if I do I always counteract its impact by adding color to my outfit. Black is a draining color for me and doesn't have the vibration I need when I work. For me and many other psychics, black can have a "downer" vibration to it. Think about funerals; aren't people sad enough already? Why wear the most negative color when you're already experiencing grief in your life? I wonder who came up with that banner idea. Let's feel more drained than we already do! Obviously, the color black is worn because of its association with "bad things" happening; in this case, death. At my funeral you will have to wear vibrant color, and there better not be a lick of black in the crowd! Trust me, I'll know! Color has great influence on us. When I go to a funeral, I never wear all black. The "dying emotion" can stick to you. I don't care if it does make you look thin. Throw on a little healing color, like pink, to counteract the negative. We tend to wear our aura colors anyway. If someone's drawn to browns, reds, and oranges, they will have a lot of Earth energy. These people are the gardeners of the world.

As for me, I'm a blue, white, and pink gal, and incidentally, I hate to garden! I love flowers and always have a vase full in my home, but don't ask me to touch dirt. It doesn't do it for me. I swear I must have been a farmer in a past life. I did this already! I really don't feel a need to put my hands in dirt again.

Some people would assume that because I'm a psychic that I also must be in touch with Mother Earth and her energy, that I must be very "earthy crunchy." Nope. Not me! I prefer to go to the mall and shop. Then, when I get back from a day of fun while my husband was gardening, I can just enjoy the scenery. He has the green thumb, and likes to wear a lot of brown and green. Now, don't get me wrong; I honor Mother Earth every day with affirmations of love and thanks. I give to her in my daily prayers. I just don't like dirt under my nails, and if that works for her than it works for me. It's kind of our little agreement.

I guess that my point is that psychics are normal people and have the same kinds of interests as everyone else. I'm not an average person only in regard to what I was "picked" to do for a living. And even with that there's a kind of normalcy to being a psychic. In order to debunk the myths around what and who we are, I want to say that not all psychics are weirdos running around casting spells. Let's take the witchery thing out of it right away. Sure, there are some psychics who choose to work that way and are O.K. with the "bad door" concept, but for the most part, all the psychics I know are very spiritual people. We work from our "highest and best good" and really understand and believe this work to be honorable and a gift to others. It's how I was raised as a young girl, with faith and spirituality. I have practiced this daily, and what Spirit has given to me I have shared with others. When we clue in to our intuition, we become a force to be reckoned with.

This is Who I Am.

Our Earth wants harmony. The big gal is talking to us and if you think she's not, well, where have you been living honey? I have a plaque in my office that I take to heart. It's an old Egyptian saying, *"The Earth is a blessing for those upon her,"* written thousands and thousands of years ago. As people living on this planet we have a duty to really grasp this concept, and remind ourselves every day not to take advantage of her.

Every morning, as I walk out to get the paper, I say a prayer about protecting Mother Earth. I thank the flowers, trees, and grass. I send love to the new blooms, the sun, clouds, rain, and even the snow. On those days when we get two feet at a whack here in Boston, I still say thank you. We forget the beauty of the Earth that lives right in our own front yard. I wonder if anyone else on my street does this. Probably not, but I do it because it makes me feel good to honor Mother Earth and her seasons. I pray for her protection and thank her for the healing she gives us all, each and every day. Switch your thinking for a minute. Get back in touch with those good manners Mom and Dad taught you. If you appreciate something, you're attentive, thankful, and polite. Be grateful to your Mother Earth! She gives us her all while never asking for anything in return. She wants balance and harmony, the same things we yearn for. Our Earth needs this too. The force of nature is so powerful. It's the source energy of love and empowerment. When you think of the Earth do you think of beauty, paradise, and tranquility? These are the words that should come to us when we catch a glimpse of her beauty.

Today when the average person thinks of Mother Earth they think of the word "use," as in "How can we use her?" Our abuse is manifesting as unchecked land development, polluted land and water, and forested areas being destroyed in the name of "progress". It's a negative pattern that has resulted in the loss of dedication to habits that are in the highest and best interest of our Mother Earth. It makes me so mad to think that humankind has been so disrespectful to her. It's like being a mother that does everything for your family but never gets a "thank you" or reward. Just expectation after expectation, day after day, and before you know, it you're burned out and just can't cope anymore. You realize you haven't colored your hair, gone out for lunch, or even read a book in ages. You just have no time, because everyone is taking from you and never giving anything back. You look in the mirror, and worse yet, you see that you're aging before your time. This is NOT GOOD. That's how I see Mother Earth. She's just damn tired and needs some pampering away from her brood of thankless kids. She needs a husband that doesn't just work to feed his family, but remembers to show appreciation to his wife so as to feed her soul. Mother Earth needs a trip to the spa and a bouquet of roses waiting for her after a cherished day to herself. She needs to come through the door and have her dinner waiting, and when she gets up from the table, someone else should be doing the dishes!

I know this sounds funny, but if you take that silly analogy and really look at how we treat the Earth, it may make better sense to you. We need to seriously change our attitude towards her! Don't treat her like a rundown, overworked mama. Treat her like the heart of the family that she is, and cherish her.

Think of Mother Earth. When is the last time you woke up in the morning and told her how beautiful she is, or thanked any of nature's elements for all they give you? I bet you are way, way overdue! Instead, we wake up, put the coffee on, grab the paper, wake the kids, get the family fed, dressed and on the bus; all within a half an hour! Hello! What happened to taking five minutes to just think and reflect on her before plowing through the day? If you're willing to change your routine just a smidgen, watch how your life will change! You'll be blessed with a beautiful energy that enlivens your day, and it won't have cost you a thing! It'll just be the special of the day, courtesy of Mother Earth.

As children, we naturally love the Earth and all it has to offer. How many pictures have you seen drawn by children with a sun smiling, beautiful bouquets of flowers, or huge trees? They're always colored with vibrant, bold hues. Kids are always so curious about how Mother Nature works. They'll ask things like "If it's raining, is she crying?" or exclaim "If it's sunny she's happy and if it's thundering, boy is she mad!" My kids once explained that very thing to me. Look how beautiful the minds of children are. So simple, yet they recognize her for who she is. They talk to her, they become artists in response to her, and they're so carefree in their love for her. We interpret a storm as something that will make for a bad commute to work instead of being grateful for the clearing that's happening because of the beautiful rain our Mother has provided. We'll still get to work, and we may even have some "down time" in the car to be thankful for. Hmm, imagine that? Of course that's only if you don't pick up your cell phone to call anyone. Please don't miss the opportunity to just be one with nature. Forget the cell or radio when you're in the car and stuck in traffic. Instead, allow yourself to just enjoy some peace and connect with your own thoughts. Take the opportunity to thank Mother Earth for the beautiful, cleansing rain that gave you a few extra minutes as you started your day. That thought alone can give you the push you need to have a good morning. Your day will also have a much better outcome if you're not grouchy because of the weather. Remember nature's connection to your soul. Mother Earth is a part of you. If you can connect with her on a daily basis, you can "phone home" to her energy and be blessed by it during any part of your life. It all boils down to the respect you have for where you live. If you have that, you can begin to have it for your soul. The words "respect" and "honor" come to mind when I think of Mother Earth. She wants for herself the same things that we want for ourselves. Appreciate your environment first thing upon awakening and you'll carry that feeling with you all day. Your world will blossom. It's all part of the shift that we're in. Embrace it.

When's the last time you touched or hugged a tree? Yes, that's right; I said "hugged." Now you're probably thinking, "This author Kelle Sutliff is whacked!" but I believe trees have a beautiful energy that can connect us to ourselves. The Native Indians believed at one point that all of our lives were connected to the trees. Think back to when you would play as a kid; if there was a tree in someone's yard, where was the action taking place? Very often, it was wherever the tree was. Kids can feel the energy around and within trees. By touching them (and yes, some of us do hug one once in a while) you'll feel lightheartedness and calmness added to your own energy. I dare you to try it! Be sure to be on the lookout for your neighbors before you start embracing trees, though. They may say "I knew she was little different. Now she's hugging trees!" When my kids were younger they would wrap themselves around, climb on, and swing from trees all the time. How lucky for them to be able to fuel themselves with that energy and not feel the need to put any judgment on it. We as adults need to do the same. We need to stop judging ourselves and honor her with our love instead.

A few years back when my daughter was in first grade, she came home from school and told me she had been talking to her best friend Talia about hugging trees, and how they give us energy. She said "Talia hugged one tree, and then another and another, and was going crazy with the energy Mom. You should have seen her!" Knowing sweet Talia, I'm sure she already had so much energy that she really didn't need to be hugging trees to get more! See how kids are so embracing of nature? They just get it, and there's no intimidation factor for them. They naturally love Mother Nature and all the gifts she gives them. Whether it's crunchy leaves to jump in, sand at the beach to build castles with, snowballs to throw at brothers and sisters, or puddles to jump in when it rains, they love it all. Mother Nature fills a child's soul. We all need to get back to that philosophy, because Earth energy is everything. Do yourself a favor and reconnect. It can be as simple as star gazing or taking a walk. Remember the saying "Take time to stop and smell the roses?" The real reason to stop is not just because they smell so darn good. It's so you'll take a moment for yourself and connect with the spirit of nature that you share with the rose. We are connected. You're not divorced from nature. You were born into her and took a soul vow to take care of her. Remind yourself of that every day. You are married to her. Just don't act like she's your domestic slave anymore. Keep all those expectations on the down low so that you won't hurt her feelings and you'll feel the peace of that mutual respect. It's time we look at this relationship in a totally different way. Can you do this as part of your soul contract with Mother Earth?

Mother Earth is pretty devastated right now. Children would describe her as being pretty angry, and that someone should be getting a TIMEOUT for making her that way! As an adult, I preach two concepts that we can use to help Mother Earth. I'm calling them the Two P's: be *Prepared*, and work on *Prevention*. These are the two of the keys needed to save our future. We're as much a part of the Earth as a branch on a tree, a seedling taking root, a flower, or a field of grass.

We need to PREPARE our homes for the environmental changes that are happening. I've done this by getting a generator for my house because of all the storms and power outages that are occurring where I live on the East Coast. You should take into consideration your own community and look how the weather has changed. We can look at Hurricane Sandy and what happened to the Jersey Shore as a wakeup call. Even with all the warnings, people tried to ride out the storm. They thought they knew better than Mother Nature, to devastating effect. I'm sure they've learned their lessons and will never do that again. We would be wise to remember that in a battle of strength, she'll always win.

Mother Nature needs PREVENTION. She needs a lot of good programs to correct the bad deeds that have been done to her, as we are quickly approaching the point of no return. If you think we can continue the abuse without repercussions, you are in for a devastating surprise. It's past time for the rehab to begin. It's more important than ever to have unity with the Earth and to quit damaging her. We should all be called into the Department of Social Services and charged with neglect. What we've done to her has been downright abusive. As the generation of healers that we are, it's time we turn our attention to her and protect her, honor her, and clean her up. Our effort to make her whole again can create a positive change for all of us, and it has to happen NOW.

How do we help heal the unease the Earth is feeling? We need to make a shift in how we think of her. We can envision, create, and implement programs to heal her. We can work with our intelligence to make better choices in an effort to prevent pollution. We can take the time to pray for a healthy Earth. Have you ever had a child or other loved one with a high temperature? What do you do? You give them Tylenol or Motrin to keep the temp down. You give them fluids, put cool compresses on their forehead and neck, watch them around the clock, and pray for their healing. If you've been a parent or a caretaker, you've been there. It's scary. You just want them to feel better, no matter what it takes.

We can apply this same concept to our planet. We can show the same love to her as we would a child with a high temperature. Your job is to soothe and protect her. It's time for you to change your recycling habits, endorse your government's "going green" bills, and take heed of new energy options, like windmills and solar power. It's time to replenish. We need to give the Earth a chance to get back on her feet. That's the prevention part that all of us can participate in. We must stop damaging her with chemicals. Would we do this to a family member? Why have we allowed this to happen to the planet that we live on? It's not healthy for her, you, or your family to use the harsh chemicals that are commonplace in most homes. It's time to wise up and go au naturale! For our Mother Earth, it will be like the feeling a woman gets when she takes off her bra, or that a man gets when he loosens his tie at the end of the day. We can no longer confine her right to be healthy with our selfishness. We've crammed our poor, dear planet into a 36 C for years, when she's really a D Cup! We can help her reach the balanced state she deserves to be in if we'll only make the choice to hold ourselves more accountable towards her.

I've done plenty of readings for people, and I can always tell when people have been damaged by chemical processes. I get a metallic taste in my mouth. It reminds me of poor Flick, whose tongue gets stuck to the flagpole in the movie *A Christmas Story*. That horrible taste in my mouth is my guide's signal that confirms for me that the person I'm reading has abused medication, illegal drugs, or has a medical diagnosis of an environmental cancer based on chemical exposure. Whenever I tell my clients what is happening with my body, I get confirmation from them that my information is correct. See how Spirit uses a medium's body to show evidence? We don't just get goose bumps once in a while. We get a whole range of physical manifestations to clue us in to what's going on with someone.

I did a reading for a woman once that had become addicted to the smell of bleach and cleaning products. If she could have bathed in it she would have. I was being shown this environmental exposure, which was from four years prior to her reading. It was at that time her addiction/obsession started. When this woman got diagnosed with breast cancer, it was already late stage and was attached to her bones. I saw this too, at the time of her reading. It was during this first reading that she was in the process of being diagnosed. I didn't share my knowledge of the late stage diagnosis of cancer that I had seen in her reading until more than a year later. Her second reading was one of the most emotional readings I've ever done in my career as a psychic. (You will have a chance to read more about Jane in a later chapter.) Mother Earth always gives me signs as to how my clients treat her and themselves, with either abuse or love. It's so much healthier to honor her than to disregard her.

In October of 2012, my psychic friend Peggy Querze was on my radio show and we were talking about planetary changes. Ironically, Mother Earth wanted to give us an example to discuss on that show. Twenty minutes before my program, Massachusetts had an Earthquake. I kid you not! It hit the East Coast and rattled us all the way up to Vermont! This part of the country NEVER gets an Earthquake! Spirit was playing a good ole' joke on us, wasn't she? As our topic of conversation on Psychic Cup of Coffee, Peggy and I were talking about paying attention to the signs and symbols out there and how psychics get these kinds of "heads up" all the time.

Peggy is very connected to the Earth channels. She pays attention to the science in relation to the changes in the Earth. Her abilities really stretch in this direction. Me, not so much, but I will get a hit once in a while. As our conversation continued on the air, she told the story about a date that she had had with an Indian chief while she was sleeping while on vacation in Sedona, AZ. Now remember, Spirit often chooses to pass through us in dreams, especially when we are someplace new. While she slept, she was aware of a thumping sound on the walls. (And no, it was not the bed rocking in the next hotel room!) She described it as the sound of tom toms or banging drums. Her husband was awakened by these noises too.

Peggy also gets taps on the face and nose when Spirit wants to get her attention, so not only was the wall getting knocked on, she was getting tapped too! By now she was up and ready to work! She saw an Indian Chief in full headdress, and he obviously wanted her attention. She was then taken into a kiva, which is an underground cave-like structure that Indians use as a sacred space in which to conduct ceremonies. Along with the Chief, she was there with a medicine man who acted as an interpreter. He told her about changes to the Earth and to prepare for meteorites that would be hitting the northern hemisphere in Russia. Then she was given the numbers 20 and 14. She assumed this meant it would happen in 2014. He also showed her the devastation that would occur due to the meteor strike, and the area that would be impacted. She saw shaking, disruptions on the ground, and the people being affected. He told her about problems concerning the Earth and Sun, and possible explosions that may lead to our power grids going out.

I know, very pleasant thoughts, right? It sounded like something straight out of a sci-fi movie! Also during this visitation, she was given an arrow and told to break it over her knee. Peggy has no connection to American Indian traditions and culture, and doesn't study it, although a lot of people who are very connected to Earth energy do. She didn't know that the breaking of the arrow is symbolic to the Sioux Indian culture and that it's often done to end a ceremony. How cool is that?

Three and a half months after Peggy had shared her dream with me, I was sitting at home when my phone rang. It was her. Without even saying hello, she excitedly blurted out "Kelle, did you hear?" "Hear what?" I responded. "A meteorite the size of an Olympic pool broke up over Chelyabinsk, Russia!" I said "Oh my God, Peg! Your dream vision came true!" Here's another interesting little tidbit. Although it didn't happen in 2014, it did happen on 02-14. Now that's some accurate psychic work! (With a little help from those beautiful American Indians of course!) Never before had there been a case of meteorites breaking up over Russia, and my friend Peggy Querze pegged it right on my radio show, *Psychic Cup of Coffee,* on October 16th, 2012.

As this story illustrates, psychics are often used by our elders to share information that can be used to protect our world. As psychics, we're enlightened, and can be used as channels to connect with a wealth of information from the other side. The information is affirmed with us energetically in order to assist us in protecting our beloved Mother Earth and ourselves.

As a collective unit, we need to continue praying for our Earth because without her, we are nothing. Prayer is the most powerful energy we have. If we all envision a beautiful, healthy gal who is cherished by all, what a beautiful world it will be! It's really as simple as that.

We also need to be prepared, because before we get to a good place with the Earth again we'll see many storm patterns coming our way. Over the coming years, these wild weather patterns will at times be quite severe. Look at the most recent storms that have hit the East Coast and the Midwest. Every time I turn on the weather channel Boston is getting nailed with two feet of snow and power outages. Many of us are tempted to say "Come on, Mother Earth! Enough is enough, already!" but I know better. The weather patterns have changed and the best we can do is prepare for more upheaval. Our lands are aligning. That's why we're seeing earthquakes, hurricanes, and volcanos erupting all over the world. We're in a major shift as the Earth tries to heal her environment and clear it all out. The most important thing you can do is to accept these types of changes as a new reality for a while. Get your flashlights and generators ready. There will be plenty of power outages to come.

Because of my connection to, and respect for our Earth, there are many things I do differently today than I've ever done in my life before. I pray for her protection before a storm hits. I tell the land, the trees, and the oceans to stay safe, to hold on tight, and to prepare for the upcoming rains, winds, or snow. Doing this is very similar to the rituals Native Americans practice to show love for their land. Most of us pray to keep our families and homes safe, but I take it to the next step and pray for our environment as well. It's the key to our survival, and more important than all the bread, milk, wine, and beer that we like to stock up on!

We have a lot of deterioration happening in our world right now due to pollution, and that has caused damage to fault lines. Earthquakes will become more commonplace and sinkholes will occur more often due to this decay. This has already begun on the East Coast.

I also want you to pay attention to the California and Oregon areas of the United States. I see the impact of waterlines rising there due to ozone neglect. All of our coastal areas can see flooding due to extreme weather. Life as we knew it twenty years ago is over. The next decade will be Mother Earth's 911. It will have the potential to bring devastation and challenges to all of us. So how do we change this? We shift our thought processes. We change our way of life. We prepare ourselves. Just as everyone has a thermometer and Tylenol in their house in case of fever, we need to be prepared to do what we can to help our Earth heal too.

We'll have many opportunities to become stronger communities through some of this devastation. Not that we want devastation. No one does. But when it does occur, we can be there for each other. Hurricane Sandy is a great example of this. Just look how that community came together during that difficult time to lend each other support. We'll also have to be there for the Earth, just as we are when anyone we love is suffering. It will really be our coming together that will lessen the pain in the coming days and allow us to heal. So get out there and do the work necessary to prevent as much of the destruction heading our way as possible. Honor our Mother Earth as our ancestors did, and pray for this ailing planet that we have taken for granted for far too long.

Teach your children

what we have taught our children:

That the earth is our Mother.

Whatever befalls the earth

befalls the sons and daughters of the earth.

Man did not weave the web of life

- he is merely a strand of it.

Whatever he does to the web

he does to himself.

- Chief Seattle

CHAPTER 3   ARE YOU READY FOR SOME CHANGE?

In case you haven't noticed, our spiritual veil has shifted. We're quickly being drawn into change in our current lives. We don't want to be who we are anymore. We suddenly don't like what choices we've made so we want to make changes. Change careers, change partners.... change, change, change, how we think and act. We want to change everything and we don't want to wait. We want to change it instantly, we want the change to happen yesterday, and we want to live in the NOW! Basically, the whole world is going through a mid-life crisis, but it's not a red sports car that everyone's longing for. (Well, maybe, but you know what I mean!) It's a new manifestation of you and your life. This new beginning is happening because the human race is finally ready for it. The bottom line is you're ready. You may not realize it but it's taken you years to get to this point. Look how much change has happened in your life in the last few years. For many of us, life's been an emotional roller coaster. You have weeded out the stuff that doesn't matter to you anymore and you're finally asking why you're here. Well you're in luck because I'm here to tell you. It's all good, and you've finally matured into your soul's purpose. That's the shift you've been feeling all along; that's another one of those layers revealed.

Today is the day to make your life what you want it to be. To embrace your soul's purpose and to decide what you really want to be when you "grow up." You should embrace this change and not be afraid of it or try to run from your destiny. Remember: you have chosen it. You're the director of this movie, this drama called "ME."

Our shift in consciousness is ever changing. It's in the ability to say "yes" and accept these new phenomena, graciously accepting your empowerment, that you will receive great things. It may not be money, a new car, or any of those types of material things that our society *thinks* create power and fulfillment. It'll be in our ability to be whole, purposeful people. Can you imagine such a thing? Just letting yourself be whole and graciously accepting the new you? This shift in consciousness that's happening is occurring now because it's needed now. For those people who aren't accepting, or fear all this change and the correction of errors, well, they'll change too, because they'll have too. You're setting yourself up for unnecessary pain if you fight it. Please don't get into the drama line. It's not a good one to be in. Run and cut into the empowerment line. It'll be the line that flows real fast!

"The flock will follow" as they say. Our shift has begun and will continue, turning our human experience around so we can become more spiritually fulfilled people. Why is this happening? It's happening because we deserve it. You may think that this is kind of a pompous answer, but it's true. Our soul's purpose deserves truth. As people we're coming of age, ready to accept our flaws and the results of our human errors. We're finally recognizing our inner voice and welcoming that voice into our lives. It's time to become true light workers and heal ourselves, so we can become a more generous, loving, and compassionate society.

Look at the barriers that have been broken down in the not so distant past, from peace talks to political and social change, in Libya, Africa, Afghanistan, and America. Walls are being torn down, cultural differences are becoming less important, and the demand for freedom is being heard all around the world. Situations like lying about weapons of mass destruction to support a war agenda by the Bush administration, or the Bengazi cover-ups that mislead the American people by the Obama administration, will not be tolerated anymore. Government misconduct is not gonna fly in the new vibrational realm. The energy is sending a big ole message; "Been there done that and not going their again!" Our elected officials need to understand this and learn from past mistakes. Not just in the United States but around the world. Leadership is changing. All the crooks of the world are being pulled away from their high ranking roles, and we're seeing a shift for the betterment of humanity. Thank God!

Society isn't just reeling, as some people are assuming. It's trying to start over fresh. Sometimes in life you have to get rid of the old so the new can come in. It's very much like clearing out your closets once a year. You dread it, procrastinate, and then finally get the adrenaline to do it. (It also helps if company is coming to stay at your house!) Wow, it sure does feel great though when you finally have everything organized! Change is the same way. You have to create the initiative to make it happen, and then keep doing it. This is all part of the plan for your soul's destination.

Not only do we feel the social changes, the weather, as I mentioned earlier, is mirroring that change as well. Extreme extremes are manifesting in everything, no matter where you live. Our souls and senses are acting the same way. Why is that? Our closets need to be cleaned. We need to hunker down and define who we are, reconnect to our goodness, and act on it. If anything gets in your way, let it fall away. It doesn't deserve to be there. The "IT" could be a person, a business, or an emotional connection to something. Whatever it is, it's not meant to stay in your life and that's OK. Remember the song from the 1970's sitcom *The Jeffersons* called "*We're Movin' on Up*"? Well you're George, and you've been invited to move into a better neighborhood!

So what is it that motivates us to make extreme change? Often it's when we lose a job, a loved one dies, we divorce our spouse, we breakup with old friends, we have a sick child, or we switch careers. Whatever the issue, it forces us to redirect ourselves. In the last few years everyone has gone through transformation. Look at your own life and ask the "Who, What, Where, When and How?" of your own psychic press release. What was your life like before, compared to NOW? Get into the nitty gritty of the problems that you may or may not have conquered, and the choices made for you by loss. Even with the tragedies you've had, I know you're a much better person today than ten years ago. That's called "shifting" and our world, both individually and globally, is going through it together. We truly are one - AMEN!

Some people understand this path better than others, and get the message without having to do as much extreme closet cleaning. Some of us have to call the 1-800-JUNK truck, and some of us just have to give a few bags to the Goodwill, but overall we're getting it.

Guess what? We've all earned an important gift by working through all that stress. It's called EMPOWERMENT. Say these words to yourself every day: "I AM EMPOWERED." Now use your psychic press release. "Who, What, When, Where, and How" have you become empowered in your life, your work, and with the people in your life? Look at how you have evolved.

Lastly, be thankful. The energy in your soul needs to be thanked. When we appreciate something, we should show gratitude. As spiritual people we've learned to be thankful for the shifts in our lives. Be thankful not only for the good, but also for the bad and the ugly. Yes, be thankful for the skills you've gained while learning to cope with stress. As crazy as that sounds, be thankful for the cancer you got, the divorce you went through, or the business that folded.

You know why? Because it has made you NEW. It's challenged you more than you could have ever dreamed. Those stresses were supposed to happen to other people though, right? Well, guess what? They really were meant for you. No one gets a pass. Life shifts to make us better souls. And by God, it will challenge us some days, just to see what we're made of. The spirituality of your soul always protects you and some days, it saves you.

Our souls are like dogs. They love us unconditionally and are by far our biggest cheerleaders. Your soul's guidance will always protect you. It always loves you and it's always so happy to see that you've learned your lessons. Be willing to creak the door open to recognize it and watch the abundance that you'll be rewarded with in your life.

I read with a positive love vibration and over the years it's become a different energy than that of ten years ago. That tells me that the veil of consciousness is thinning. We need to accept our intuitive sight. We all have it. It's just a question of whether or not we want to accept the gift of inner wisdom. It talks to us daily. Are *you* willing to listen?

The universe today wants us to listen to our inner voice. It's time to pay attention to the signs and symbols we get every day from our loved ones, our guides, and our angels as they talk to us. They are all too common not too. Ask for signs, and when you get them, act on them. How many times do we see references from our loved ones? Seeing a car like your dad's, hearing just the right song on the radio, seeing the same numbers again and again, or the lamp that flickers in your home when you think of a departed loved one, are just a few examples of how spirit talks to you. You need only ask for a sign and then wait for it. All energy is used to get our attention.

The Purple Dinosaur Theory

If you have a dilemma in your life, use my Purple Dinosaur Theory. ("First she has me hugging trees, and now I'm looking out for dinosaurs. I know this medium is crazy!" is what I'm sure you're all saying to yourselves... Not true! Just listen to my example!)

I always tell my clients to use the following little tool. You all have this team of loved ones around you to guide you, so think of a question or situation you want help with in your life. Now, be specific and think of a symbol you want to see; for example, a purple dinosaur. If you're meant to trust your hunch about this situation, you'll see nine Barneys that day. You'll see him on sheets and comforters, on magazines and lunchboxes. You'll even see the *word* "dinosaur" somewhere!

Remember, you've created the intention with your intuition, which is the vibrational link to the other veil/side of energy. You've raised the bar so they can give you an answer. When I act as a conduit when giving a reading, I'm raising my energy level to meet the energy level of the soul I'm connecting with so they can give me information. You can do this just as easily with symbols in order to get clarification about situations in your life.

Recently, I had a client come for a reading. I explained my "Purple Dinosaur Theory" and she called me to tell me she had used it. She had a very healing reading. When she came to see me she had a lot of residual anger concerning wills and trusts among her family. She chose a pink car as her symbol connecting her to her deceased parents. Her question was whether or not she was doing the right thing by entering into a lawsuit regarding the will. On the drive home, she was looking at all the cars on the highway. The closest color she saw was maroon. Feeling disappointed, she went to bed. The next morning she woke up, stepped out of bed, and tripped on her daughter's PINK Barbie car. That's how Spirit gives us answers when we ask for symbols from them. This poor girl had to literally step on her pink car, barely awake, to get her sign, but she got it, didn't she?

I was having a day of deep grieving after my father died. I said out loud "Dad, give me a sign that you're okay." That day I went to my local grocery store. I picked up a bag of flowers for my house and threw them into the cart, which is part of my usual routine. I returned home, unloaded the groceries, and put the flowers in a vase. As I was arranging the bouquet, a flower literally bonked me on the head! I looked at the flower and it was a Bells of Ireland wildflower, which cost about three dollars a stem. How it got mixed into my $6.99 bouquet, I have no idea. (Well, I guess I really do.) We had Bells of Ireland flowers in all the flower arrangements at my dad's funeral. We're Irish and he was a true Irishman and proud of his heritage. My father hit me over the head with a flower that he knew I would recognize, giving me the answer that yes, he's around, and of course, he's okay.

Some of the most symbolic messages are given to us when we find something that had belonged to someone we loved. As an example, I once got a note from a client on her birthday. She was having a really tough day. We can all get a bit melancholy during special events. These occasions can really make us acutely aware of the absence of our loved ones. As she was looking in a drawer for a thank you card to send to a friend, she came across an old birthday card her mom had given her. It was a card telling her daughter Happy Birthday and that she loved her. The intention and the link were there and mom managed to connect to her daughter, didn't she? Her mom was right there, wishing her a Happy Birthday. Spirit always knows just when they're needed. We could all have better birthdays if we would just look for those signs from Spirit. It's an extra layer of connection that they provide for us.

The universe's whispers are all around us. They are there to guide us, and we need to pay attention to their symbolism. Here's another great example. I was in my kitchen at 6:30 in the morning, and my daughter was getting ready to go on a ski trip to Quebec. (Don't all thirteen year olds do this type of field trip in middle school?) I was excited that the kids were being given such an amazing opportunity! Thank goodness for Mr. Givens, who came out of retirement just to take these kids on this adventure. What an awesome teacher! We were in a hurry, as is usual in my house, and Haley was making a cup of tea. She always saves the back of the tea bag. (If you drink Salada brand tea, you'll know they have quirky sayings or funny blurbs on the tags.)

She and I were talking about my manuscript and when it would be done, when she said "Mom, look at this. I think this is for you." I read the tea tag and it said **"Pearls of Wisdom are very rare."** I had just co-written the book *Pearls of Wisdom - 30 Inspirational Ideas to Live Your Best Life Now!* On that day I was planning on writing the last chapter for this book. I know in my heart that this one is going to knock it out of the park because of the insights in it. Imagine all that symbolism over breakfast! Here's another way the symbolism played out. My chapter in *Pearls* was called *Daily Cup of Calm,* and these signs came while I was sharing a cup of tea with my daughter. Isn't that cool?

On the drive to the bus Haley said to me "That sure was a coinky-dink, Mom." I said "You're right Hale, someone is certainly giving me a message. Thanks for making that cup of tea this morning!" and we both just smiled.

So what did I do with this symbolism? I wrote all day that Saturday, (in the time between driving the kids around of course) and guess what? I finished this book. That tea tag is in my wallet, and will stay there forever because "Pearls of Wisdom are always very rare." I think Oprah calls these kinds of experiences her "Aha!" moments. You can call it a message, a sign, or even a coinky-dink, but whatever your name for it is, know that when it happens it's a gift. Use the symbol and its insights to fulfill something within you because it's coming from a higher source. I like to call that source "God's heart."

You will see many messages show up from your loved ones if you'll only stay on the lookout for them. Some may say "Oh, that's just a coincidence." I'm here to tell you that *nothing* is coincidence. It's just another example of how spirit uses signs and symbols to get our attention.

People are so busy today that they may need to hear it, see it, and feel it, sometimes a few times, to realize the important aspect of the message. I could say some people are clueless when it comes to psychic messages, but I'll be polite and just say that they're "slower to get it." If everyone would just take a few minutes to relax, listen to their hearts, and see the symbolism around them, they would feel so empowered. Once you start to do this there's no turning back. You'll open a door that will lead to a WHOLE (see the word I am using?) new you, even if that change brings with it a purple dinosaur!

I've been reading for well over fourteen years now. I've taught classes on mediumship. I work as a psychic detective. I'm an author and host a national radio show. I'm telling you all this because I think it will show that I just might know a little bit about the importance of energy work and keeping yourself grounded. I really, really do get how this energy thing works, and I want you to get it too.

The most important thing you can do for yourself is to connect with your INNER self. By doing so you'll be able to focus your inner energy which will bring peace and serenity to your day. Just how do you do this? Grab your "Psychic Cup of Coffee" every morning. Looking for some calm? It's right there. Compared to the real java we grab every morning, this cup is far, far better and should be the real start to everyone's day.

Why? Because it will protect you and plant you firmly in the "I AM" present moment. Think about how you make a pot of coffee. You use a filter and pure, clear water so there are no impurities. Your psychic cup of coffee does the same. It purifies you to filter out the gook in your life and creates a barrier so the bad stuff can't get in. When you're done with this simple exercise, man, do you feel good! This simple routine teaches you how to ground yourself, clears the negative energy away from your body, and jumpstarts you for the day YOU want to have. Imagine that, a day for Y-O-U. It creates a pattern in your life so the routine of grounding becomes second nature. Those "energy junkies" can't get into your space, because you won't let them. We all know people who just want to use us, and unfortunately, we often let them. This behavior isn't good for anyone, and over time it wears on your soul and the layers become weakened. We all have these situations in our lives which can be difficult to avoid. But it's important that when we start to feel overwhelmed, we let it go. It happens to all of us, but there comes a time when you have to put your hand up and energetically say "STOP!" It's the protection you need from emotional vampires that want to suck you dry. This is just what the doctor should order for you to get better!

You'll be way clearer in your decision making and less anxious. And the best thing about this little gift I'm teaching you is that it will make you happier. Now, who wants in?

There may be days when you'll want to do this more than once, because, well... life is life. Just by watching your thoughts you can give yourself a shot of good ole' groundedness. You can do it at work, at the playground with the kids, or before a sales presentation while stuck in traffic. Better yet, how about in your driveway before you bring your crummy day into your home? Clear it all away before you walk into the house. Don't bring any of your negative stuff into your sacred space! This is your stress free zone and you need to honor it. Please don't abuse it with bad energy.

Imagine the middle fingers you could avoid flipping while commuting! My son is getting his driver's license this year and I really think this exercise for calm should be a on the driving test, just like "What does an octagonal, red sign mean?" (Correct answer: Stop) Imagine what could happen if we added a question like "How do you keep calm before you drive?" (Correct answer: Ground) See? We'd have so many more patient drivers on our roads!

Driving could become a happy event instead of the stressful one it usually is due to tense and neurotic drivers. We've all felt it, even me. Hey, I'm the mom of three teenagers now, living the "mini-van dream," trying to get across town to drop someone off to practice, an art lesson, or a game. Oh, and let me add; usually all at the same time! I get the importance of grounding myself, just as I advise everyone else to do. If everyone took a few minutes to do this, we wouldn't see as many of the blank stares or dazed looks that we tend to have while racing to get to our destinations. We'd be able to have a few more laughs and smiles on our faces instead. Think "peace" instead of "that guy driving in front of me is a jerk!"

I've always told my clients that the most important gift we can give to ourselves is to connect with our physical and spiritual aspects. By combining these together into a daily practice, you will have the recipe for calm.

I know, easier said than done, but if you practice you'll see what I mean. I've been showing this exercise to all of my clients for fourteen years. I open up every reading with this same routine. I also show people the importance of grounding before meditation.

It's sometimes hard to believe how ungrounded and kinetic people are today. It's become acceptable in our society, and that's not okay. Not anymore. It's time to claim your balance back. Let everyone else be agitated if they want to be, but as of today, you're going to choose not to be. It's the first question I ask before I read for someone. "Do you ground or meditate every day?" Some will say "No" but many fib and say "Yes," but I know they really don't. I'm a psychic, remember? I know when people aren't telling me the truth. My kids will tell ya, it kinda stinks growing up in my house. There's not much they can get away with. Oh well …

In order to keep our mind, body, and spirit working in true harmony, we shouldn't neglect quiet, grounding meditation time but most of us do. It's really very abusive when you think about it. We may go to a gym to work out for our health, but then we come home and create a toxic environment by being hotheaded or curt with our words. I can't stress enough how important it is to learn the power of "Now Energy." We all have access to it and can use this new layer of soul to enhance our lives. It will benefit you and your intention to work for your highest and best good in many, many ways.

You have a choice to be whole or not. If you choose to be whole for the day, than you'll have the alignment needed to create the best day possible. Again, we all have a choice, and if you don't want to protect your energy, avoid chaos, and create abundance in your life, so be it. No problem. But know that eventually you'll be forced to change, due to the Earth changes around you. As I said before, Mother Earth's energy is reeling, and it's shaking up our world, our economy, and our emotional states. You don't have to be an expert in energy work to pick that up. We're at war, we have an unstable economy, and we have leadership that's not leading, but dictating. We have a lot of work to do on ourselves to keep from getting sucked into this kinetic cycle.

Think of the weather lately; earthquakes, floods, high temperatures, crazy winters, wildfires, and tsunamis. Did I cover all those Earth elements? There are a lot of shifts happening around us. Another place they're happening is with our economy. Notice all the foreclosures on homes, stock markets crashing, companies closing, and more and more people out of work. This isn't a healthy formula for any of us. That's a lot of heaviness, isn't it? I had to take a deep breath after writing this because it's so negative. When I exhaled, I sent healing light to all those issues.

This is big, heavy stuff, and neither you, I, or our Mother Earth deserve it. Again, think about all of the chaos in the world right now. It's like trying to live through an earthquake. If you're not holding on to something, you won't survive it. The person hanging on tight survives. That's how it works. So I'm telling you now, grab a hold and don't let go! All *that* energy affects *your* energy, and you have to protect your energy field to keep from being negatively affected by it all. Instead though, we often foolishly leave our energy field open, for anything or anyone to grab. This is an important message from Spirit; yet another layer for us to understand. We need to cradle our energetic fields, and that's the energetic bottom line.

So how can you get a handle on all those negative situations? Grab your balance as if you're life depended on it because, in reality, it does. When we command ourselves to do something, our body follows that lead. It allows our intuitive self to be our guide. Let me tell you a secret. You have access to it every day. It's a gift you can give to yourself so that you can be in charge. If you want to be rid of the chaos in your life then you have to have peace in your soul. If you want to attract the healthy good and best towards you, then take control of your thoughts and energy and "play nice" with them. Don't let anyone or any circumstance violate your energy field. It's that simple. Your "Psychic Cup of Coffee" will create a barrier to people who are "energy junkies" and the bad situations they create. All of a sudden people learn to behave around you. They can no longer tap into or use you. At some point you start to say no, and those people stop asking for favors. Isn't that a fabulous thing, not to be used up by others? Practice this, and learn to say "No" to the things that don't serve your soul. It will make all the difference to your own sense of peace.

So, are you ready to get this new cup of calm into your life? I am too. Let's get started on creating the new you, preferably right now! First off, go throw the coffee together and sit down in your quiet spot, wherever that may be. Try to make it somewhere that you will be undisturbed for three minutes. That's all it takes, just three minutes. Your prize when you're done will be that morning cup of java. O.K., now that you're sitting, place your feet flat on the ground. Take a few deep breaths. Close your eyes and begin to see a spiritual white light, or any color that resonates with you. It could be pink, blue, green, or orange. Just pick a color that you feel speaks to your consciousness. As the light showers above you and hits the crown of your head, surrender your fears and worries, and state your intentions for your day. Say things like: "I stay calm with my kids." "I am closing that business deal today." "I am a calm driver." "I am cured of cancer." These affirmations will be different for everyone, so be very focused and specific about whatever your intentions are for that day.

Always, always state it in the present tense. By doing this you get the "I AM" momentum. You give the universe the green light to make it happen today. Not ten years from now, or two months, or twelve days, but today. For example, don't say "I hope this is going to happen." Hope can give the universe the yellow light, the pause to yield to a later time. You want your energy and intention to work instantly, so remember to say your intentions in the present tense and envision them happening right now.

As you keep pulling this light down through your body, picture it passing from the top of your head to your forehead, then throat, heart, stomach, knees, and feet. All these energy points are called chakras. These chakras hold energy. If any are out of alignment, we can experience it as illness in that part of the body. Remember that mind-body connection? Well, there it is.

As you keep envisioning this healing spiritual light descending through your body, state your intentions (prayers) for the day. When you do this you purify your system, protecting your energy field and dissolving any of that pent up gook I mentioned earlier.

As this magnetic, spiritual, light showers through you, envision your feet solidly on our blessed Mother Earth, grounding you in the power of your own self.

Envision a tree trunk, a root, or an anchor; whatever visually helps you plant yourself and your energy for the day that lies ahead. Draw on the protective white (or colored) light the way a flower draws on the sun for growth. It bathes itself in it, absorbing all the good in nature. You are the same way. You need to absorb the good and let the good happen.

Now open your eyes.

That's it. In those few moments you will have created calm, abated the chaos, attracted abundance for your highest and best good, created harmony, balanced your physical body and spiritual self, and protected your energy. Yes, you own it and no one else can take it away. You have just had your morning cup of calm. Now go get that other cup. Your coffee is done.

Here is a picture of the chakras of the body:

Crown Chakra
Honors Spiritual
Connectedness

Third Eye Chakra
Honors the Psychic

Throat Chakra
Honors Communication

Heart Chakra
Honors the Heart

Solar Plexus Chakra
Honors the
Life Force

Splenic Chakra
Honors the
Creative

Root Chakra
Honors the Earth

CHAPTER 5

DON'T JUST JUMP, DIVE INTO YOUR SPIRITUAL POOL

"We are not human beings having a spiritual experience.

We are spiritual beings having a human experience."

Pierre Teilhard De Chardin

My husband Tom and I were both raised Catholic, and both attended twelve years of parochial school. Tom was even an altar boy. Our children have also been raised Catholic, but "with a twist." I attend a Spiritualist Church too. This has allowed them to diversify their thoughts about religion, what spirituality is, and what universal law principles are, while still having a foundation through an organized religion. It's important to have some type of foundation on which to rest your faith and which also gives you peace. It's especially important for our children.

That's also how I grew up. My mom was a practicing Methodist and my dad was a practicing Catholic when they married. Back then, some sixty years ago, when people had an interfaith marriage (and one of those faiths was Catholic) you had to sign an agreement to raise your children Catholic in order to be married in the Catholic Church. Sometimes even then you would have to get married at the side altar. Can you imagine? Thank goodness, my folks were "good enough" to march down the center aisle when they married! That kind of control is somewhat gone from the rules of most religions today. Society has changed for the better, and most people wouldn't put up with that anymore. That said, even today according to Papal Law, the Catholic Church still makes you sign an agreement to raise your children Catholic. But now they let you walk down the center aisle and don't shun the poor soul you married whose religious beliefs are different than yours. They also no longer have to convert. The world is making some big strides in this area. It's going to take a while, but we are getting closer to wholeness. We all just have to have patience a little longer!

Here's some more positive news. We're all good enough, no matter what our religion or spiritual beliefs are. We're touched with love and directed by God. Spirit doesn't care about all those hardcore rules that organized religion can place on us. They just care about you, and how you treat yourself and others. That's the bottom line when it comes to Spirit consciousness.

As a society of faith, we have lessened dogmatic thinking and are embracing a new way of being. Spirit tells me that this way of thinking is much more evolved and healthier too. It's time to immerse yourself in your spiritual pool. Jump on in and evolve! This is not the time to be stand offish and vulnerable. It's the time to take a chance on your soul's spirituality. Your soul is like a rock. It's strong and will always support you. This is another layer that you need to understand about your intuitive self. Your mind is looking for peace, and guess what? Your soul is ready to provide that to you. You can have a great marriage between the two of you, but just as in any marriage, you have to work at it to get it right.

In my home, it's important to me that my children have faith as their foundation. They are conscious and good little souls who can think outside the box and be sensitive to others. Shouldn't this be the basis of any healthy religion? Even the new Pope agrees! If you practice faith, love for others, and always remember that "the hand that gives gathers" you'll be standing on solid ground. I have that simple reminder on a sign that's hanging in my bedroom. It's the first inspirational thought I have at the start of my day. I keep words on all my walls as reminders to me as to how to live my best life. You can't go into a room in my home and not get a little inspiration; not even the bathroom!

The golden rules in life are the "Universal Axiom" that my friend and co- author Stacey Goforth writes about in *Pearls of Wisdom - 30 Ways Inspirational Ways to Live Your Best Life Now!* The golden rule we all know is "Do unto others as you would have them do unto you." It's widely thought that this is a Christian teaching, but it's actually a fundamental teaching in many faiths. Stacey broke those beautiful golden rule words down over fifteen faiths to show it's commonality among religions. She included the Baha'i Faith, Buddhism, Judaism, Islam, Native American, and several spirituality based teachings, just to name a few.

We forget that don't we? We can get so caught up in the righteousness of our own religious beliefs that we need to be reminded that we all work as one WHOLE consciousness in this world. We need to take the fear out of faith and let another layer fall away from our misdirected thoughts. True Spirit teaches that we're all just ONE. This is a reminder that we really need to understand and embrace this concept. Our faith is no better than anyone else's. "We are in the spirit of being spiritual people" is something that I like to say.

I always crack up when I visit old cemeteries and there's a Catholic side, a Protestant side, and a Jewish side. Do you really think souls don't hang out with each other in Heaven? I'm here to enlighten you to the fact that they do. They're all mixed together and in the same loving energy field. I know this because when I link in a reading to whoever wants to connect to you, they give a message in that moment. They don't wait for Passover, Christmas, or Ramadan. They don't refuse to show up because it's not their day to give messages. They come in as a unit, religious beliefs aside, just for you. This means that we need to be together too. We should strive to have no division in our communities. Just practice

"The Golden Rule" principals, and I believe you'll be rewarded in the next realm of consciousness.

So, why all this talk about spirituality? Because as a psychic medium, I *have* to have a spiritual foundation in order to do this work. In my opinion the psychic medium that doesn't, isn't the whole package. If you don't have some form of spiritual belief, how on Earth can you connect to the love vibrations of those that have passed on? Sharing their messages is how they show that there is continuity to life. My work is never fear based, partly because of my faith. It's always love based, and often with a splash of humor, because Spirit is funny! That's where the energy comes from.

It always comes from the GOOD.

There's no reason to get your undies in a bunch thinking that this kind of work comes from an evil place. It just doesn't come from that space, plain and simple. I work with the highest vibration I can and that vibration is always LOVE. Think about it. Without love, how would the energy come through? On some kind of a hate train? If so, why would I want to be a part of that? I wouldn't.

Don't be afraid to climb aboard! It's all coming from the love train, full of healthy, great energy!

For those of you that know me now, or will come to know me after reading this book, do you really think a mom of three, wife, PTO board member, teacher and volunteer, would work with an evil energy to do a reading? Nope, not me. I have too much to lose for myself, my family, and my reputation. I've never seen this work as negative in any way. I've only experienced it as healing, and I've seen this simple truth in action, again and again, with people suffering loss. The pain one feels after losing a loved one to death is intense, and takes a lot of work of conscious effort to heal. I have clients who are young adults, all the way up to people close to ninety. Of the thousands and thousands of people I have read for over fourteen blessed years, all have left their readings with a sense of relief and an awareness of how Spirit works. They feel hope, love, and humor, (yes, humor!) because Spirit is known to have a laugh or two during a reading. A reading is never meant to be doom and gloom. It's meant to be uplifting and rewarding.

These are the emotions that people most often feel after I read for them.

That's not to say I never have clients afraid to have a reading. I often hear "Don't tell me anything bad." As with anything, it's all in the presentation. If I see a tragedy, like an accident that's going to happen, I'm asked "Can you give a warning to someone so they can change the outcome?" Sure I can. When spirit comes through to give a message and wants someone to be careful about something, I encourage them to listen. Spirit wants to protect them from harm. When you were a child and you went somewhere, your mom would say "Be careful." That reminder was to make you think about what you were doing and to stay aware of your surroundings, right? It's the same with Spirit.

My mom still reminds me of this and I'm forty-eight years old and live out of state! It's a good habit. Spirit and its energy have good habits too. Take this as another layer revealed to you. They give us reminders through readings for us to be careful and to be aware of our surroundings. Is there anything wrong with that? They're doing their job, working to protect you. It's "safety first."

It's what I teach my kids, what schools teach, and what society teaches, so why wouldn't Spirit teach it too? The answer is, they do. Don't fear a warning, or as I like to call it, "a heads up." Keep yourself aware and take the opportunity to have the power to change. Muster up the courage to dive into your spiritual pool!

I dare you to change how you think. In the 1970's when I grew up, there was a commercial for LIFE cereal. There were two brothers looking at this new box of cereal on the breakfast table. The older brother is coaxing his little brother, saying "Hey, Mikey! Try it you'll like it!" He wanted to make sure someone else tested it out first. I'm saying the same thing to you.

Take a chance on seeing how the Spirit in all of us works. Learn more about universal law principles like "The Golden Rule" and how they operate in your life. I will guarantee you that just like the older brother who exclaims "He likes it!" when Mikey eats his cereal, that when it comes to Spirit, you'll like it too. The universe's energy will give you the green light to try new things. Without inspiration, many people have seen the world as half empty. Well, not anymore! Your cup will "runneth" over! You'll be filled to the top with this new spiritual energy. There will be no halves at all running around, only wholes.

We create our intentions with hopes for the distant future. From here on out, we'll be replacing them with the NOW presence. We're too humble to believe we deserve good now, when in fact you're entitled to have good in your life instantly. All the religions that use God's wrath as punishment will have to kiss that thought goodbye and change. If you choose to have faith in yourself, faith in God/Spirit/Universe, and faith in humanity, what will come back to you is always for your soul's good. It will never cause harm.

The energy transforms you and honors you. It always does and always will, but you'll only feel it if you acknowledge it. Let it in and pretend you're like Mikey. Quit living your life in ambivalence. If you choose to live with this type of energy and attitude, you'll never get out of your own way and create your best. As a mother and cheerleader to your spirituality, please listen and stop the pity party right now! Think positively! As my sweet daughter Haley says "It's all about the positivity!" I also often hear from her "It's ALL GOOD Mom! It's ALL GOOD!" She even tells her soccer coaches that it's all good when her team is losing in a tournament. She tells her friends the same if they're having a tough day. Please take a cue from this smart fourteen year old, because she's right on. Your spirit wants you to work on your positivity too!

One of the many steps to your spiritual growth is to honor yourself. The practice of respecting your Spirit creates the abundance of whatever you desire to be attracted into your life. It can be a new career, conceiving a baby, or getting good marks to get into college. The universal principle concept creates healthy intention so that you can receive what you want right now. Get started shifting your attitude because this is how it works.

As a for instance, let's say you want to change your job. Here's what you'd do….

1. Envision your new job. Envision the pay, work environment, even the start date.

2. Ask the universe with your intention being "For the highest and best good, for myself and my family whom I provide for, I am in this new career by (pick your date)."

3. Affirm your desire every day.

4. Bless yourself with your intentions and watch how your circumstances change.

You will be full of the energy that creates greatness. New people, headhunters, old bosses and friends, and new opportunities will come onto your path to help make your dream a reality. Now you're on the flipside of just how universal law can create a heck of a lot of good. It can also create disparity and negative situations. There is a "balance" or an "out of balance" to everything you do. If you work within your spiritual pool and it's full of muck and negativity, your desired outcome will not happen for you. If you clean out your pool and rid your soul layer of negative thoughts and disparity, you open a door to possibilities.

As I tell my clients all the time, our energy and the universe are working at warp speed and whatever you think, feel, say, and do happens as quick as a wink. If you still want to go down negativity road be cautious, because you'll most likely be kicked with some big wake up calls. That "Debbie Downer" attitude will attract to you what you don't want. It'll be your worst friend for a long time. We all know people that are always depressed and feeling sorry for themselves. Their favorite song is "Boo hoo, poor me." Know this; Your "Boo hoo, poor me" routine sticks around and has a party with your psyche. "Like always attracts like." My advice to you is to stay positive. That way all good things will be attracted to you. Remember Haley's comments about positivity? That's how it works. It really is that simple. This is often why energetically we can't stay with people. Friends, family, or even spouses fall to the wayside. The reason is because you've changed your plateau of energy and your vibration has changed for your soul's betterment. This is another layer revealed to you. You don't need to be discouraged by this. Be encouraged. This is the job of your soul. If your situation in life changes, (and that includes the people you hang around with) go with it. You'll look back at your circumstances with compassion and healing, and with many thanks for the lessons they gave you. The best part is that you'll be a more illuminated person in the future.

The soul's reflection is amazing. When I see clients a year later for a second reading, I can see the affect that the advice of their loved ones and spiritual guides has had on them. They have healed, and beautiful change has manifested because of it. They've been transformed because they were brave enough to let their spiritual pool open up and work for them. There's nothing better than the advancement of your soul.

People need to remember that when our loved ones pass, they're in a spiritual pool of their own. That doesn't mean they're no longer our parents, kids, friends, aunts, uncles, or cousins though. Death doesn't change any of that. The role of that person in our lives stays with us. Their compassion, love, and belief in us persist. They're still influencing us and they are the best cheerleaders we have.

People often think that Spirit become these great mystics, communicating from the other side. Nope. They keep the same energy and act as they did in life. The only difference is that sometimes they soften, which is a good thing. The people who did harmful things to a loved one often come through with love and apologies for my clients. This connection always shows me how the soul grows on the other side and that life is one big continuum. I always say it's easier to learn your lessons here on Earth than on the other side. You really have to work harder over there to correct your mishaps. It's best to get it right the first time whenever you can.

Your passed loved ones want to hear from you so don't stop the communication. They're around you to guide you and they too see the powerful force of LIFE. They once had it themselves here on Earth. In their new dimension their soul energy is transformed, but it's still LIFE. It's just in a dimension we haven't felt yet. Is it fear based? No. It's always love based and from a wonderful kind of space. The best way I can describe this energy is to liken it to the first time you hold a baby, a new puppy, or anything that loves you back unconditionally. That's the vibration our deceased loved ones exist in 24/7. How lucky are they? I had a loved one come through once and he said, "It feels just great here. You can't imagine Kelle. There's so much love." I believe him. I feel a tiny glimpse of it when I'm the conduit giving a message to someone during a reading. I have the best job in the world! I'm able to give love, closure, healing, and words of comfort to my clients from their loved ones. The soul gives it to them through its highest and best, good intention. I'm so blessed to be able to participate as the messenger.

You think our energy runs fast? The other side's vibe never runs on empty! It's such a high vibration that I have to meet it halfway in order to work with them as the conduit.

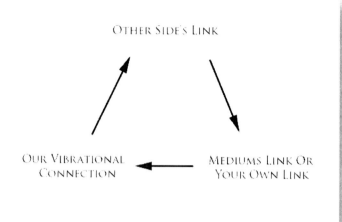

OTHER SIDE'S LINK

OUR VIBRATIONAL
CONNECTION

MEDIUMS LINK OR
YOUR OWN LINK

The vibration connects so that we can all work together, because the end goal is to get the message out, right? We're all still intertwined within our spiritual makeup. Whether it's here on Earth or with our loved ones on the other side, our love vibration stays between us. It never leaves the link. We're always connected. The link we have with the people we love never, ever changes. It's blessed and honored within our spiritual pool and a part of all that we are or will ever be.

There's a message in the word LIFE that we all need to understand from our deceased loved ones. Their message to us is this: Live It Fully Everyone. They don't want us to NOT live life. Don't pine and anguish for years after their death. Celebrate them and pray to them. Their souls will grow from these prayers. This is by far the best medicine you can give to your passed loved ones. They get showered with healing and completeness through your prayer. Even the nasty people that showed up in your life here on Earth need prayer. Some of those souls are so thirsty for it that when they are prayed for they drink it up as if they'd been lost in the desert. Prayer is always healing because it simply transforms us. It doesn't matter what religion you are. The message I've heard, over and over again throughout the years from passed souls, is to remember LIFE –

Live It Fully Everyone.

The pool is waiting.

Get your suit on and get ready to swim!

CHAPTER 6

MEDIUMS ARE MUCH MISUNDERSTOOD

When *All Hallow's Eve* approaches in October, the world of spirits, ghosts, witches, and the supernatural are all around us. For the most part, it's all in good fun. Despite the festive nature of Halloween, that time of the year always makes me reflect on how misunderstood the work of a psychic medium is. I'm constantly defending my work and weeding out the unsavory concepts that pervade the psychic medium industry.

Sure, there are people who appreciate and understand what it is that I do. But there are many others who view this work as some sort of quackery or witchery hogwash. TV shows and movies that sensationalize the work of mediums aren't exactly helpful in my real world. Shows like *Long Island Medium* tell the stories of how a medium connects and gives messages, but would you find *this* medium, ME, walking up to someone in a coffee shop, grocery store, or while doing yoga and blabbing off a message to a stranger who hasn't asked me for it? NO WAY! I think it makes the format of the show look a little whacky. In my psychic rulebook, this work always has to have some basic boundaries in place. Rule number one is not to invade someone's space unless they have invited you into it. I think *TLC* and *The Long Island Medium* program has done a disservice to other people in my profession by deceiving their American audiences into believing that mediums just bump into random strangers and start reading them. It's that kind of image that mediums who do this work with a spiritual basis have to constantly work against. No one person can be "on" and doing this work full time. Who the heck would want to be a psychic medium 24/7? Does an accountant or nurse work 24/7? No, they don't, so why would a medium? If Teresa Caputo, or any psychic for that matter, stays "on" all the time, I can't help but believe that they'll suffer from burnout. In my experience, it's very unhealthy for our energy.

One evening on my radio show, I was discussing the misconceptions that the *Long Island Medium* program has created for my industry. It's really funny to ponder that psychics now think they can go grab people out of the blue and say "Hey! I have your mother here and she has a message for you!" Now, anyone who shouts this to you and gets your attention has a 50/50 chance of getting it right. This hooligan practice has now become commonplace. Such bullcrap! From what I hear, this has become an actual problem in New York, as well as other parts of the country. Con artists are now practicing this type of mediumship and mimicking the show, grabbing people in stores and supermarkets and "acting" the part of Teresa Caputo. This is a very unhealthy practice, as now the public believes that this is how real psychic mediums work. We're definitely feeling the fallout from this show on *TLC*.

I was always taught, as other mediums I know were also taught, that you should never intrude on someone's space. You have to have permission both verbally and energetically in order to read for someone. It's similar to when someone rings your doorbell. You always ask who it is, and only when you feel safe do you open the door. You wouldn't just let any stranger into your home. If they demanded that you open the door, RIGHT NOW, would you say "Come on in"? You would do no such thing, so why on earth would you allow just anyone who says their psychic to invade your space?

No person can be grounded when they're reading like this. The person getting accosted is likely to be thinking "What the heck? Who is this crazy person grabbing at me in the sample isle at Costco?" Do you really think your mother wants to communicate to you like that, and would she do it in Costco? (Unless she was a big shopper of course, and then that may be significant as evidence!)

The message that I and many other mediums want to stress to you is that this method is not a polite or spiritual practice, and generally not how a true medium reads. Usually these hooligans are randomly making a money grab by going after people in this way. So please remember, if you're in a Costco getting free samples (or anywhere else for that matter) and you get approached, say "No thanks" and walk away. These are people that may be trying to rip you off. This work, and my mission, as with many qualified mediums, is to work with integrity. I, for one, have made making sure this happens my life passion. If you don't work with the right elements, it really mucks it up for the rest of us.

My advice is to get referrals from people you know before a reading. That's really how most of my clients come to me. When you need a cleaning lady, a good plumber, or a great builder, you always look for a reference. It's the same in my line of business. Ask around and make sure your source is trustworthy.

I believe I'm a normal person, whatever that means. I'm married, raising three great kids, and taking care of a home and business. This is both hectic and wonderfully rewarding. My days are busy, and I find myself doing the same kind of balancing act between work and family that thousands of other people across the country do every day. While I can't tell you what the lottery numbers will be on Friday, I can connect you to a passed loved one and deliver a message from them to you. Some people may think that that is truly winning the lottery.

Mediumship is a form of healing therapy, and the idea that we can communicate with spirits has existed for centuries. The movement known as Spiritualism was widely introduced in the United States in the mid-19th century, and gained tremendous popularity in the early 20th century. During the Civil War, on both sides of the country North and South, mediums were used to connect to dead soldiers to make sure they had crossed over and were all right. The role of the medium picked up after World War I and II for the same reasons. The emphasis of the work today is to show spiritual healing and the continuing of life.

Psychic mediums have many gifts besides reading for clients. They're used in business, in healing, and in law enforcement to help solve crimes and find missing persons.

I have often worked on cases with the Cold Case Collaborative out of Boston University and National Organizations like LostNMissing, and Find Me. I also work with families privately investigating missing person cases or murder cases. I'm compelled to find the evidence that can lead to a resolution. My intuition is very strong when representing a dead or living missing person. I'm just like a police detective. I intuitively go over and over cases. Sometimes I don't sleep well at night because I've failed to "click" myself off, only to wake up in the middle of the night seeing the child, mother, daughter, or son who is missing, giving me evidence. Sometimes I get clues to a case when I am in a dream state. Other times it happens as I'm going through a routine day.

Here's the difference between me and the detectives. They have all the hard facts, the files, DNA evidence, and a database of perpetrators to research. I only have a name, the location where the victim went missing, and their picture. All of my evidence comes from Spirit and the missing person. I intuitively fill in my own database with information, and so the psychic press release begins. Essentially, I help the dead assist the living solve the cases.

I'm convinced that we all have the gift of intuitiveness. For some it may register more strongly than for others, as another part of their soul layer is revealed. We're all gifted with psychic ability though, every one of us. The difference is whether or not we choose to accept our gift and cultivate it. I believe everyone needs to listen to the hunches and warning signs that their intuition can provide daily. It's no secret that relying on what is often called your "gut instinct" is actually one of the most powerful intuitive tools available to each one of us.

As I've worked as a psychic medium over the years, my training has served me well and I've helped many people. I continue to wish and hope for more understanding about what it is that I and others can do. To be a psychic medium is a choice, but it's also a gift. No one grows up and says, "I want to be a Psychic Medium." You accept this work as part of your path, just as I did while making baby formula in my kitchen fourteen years ago.

On that day I accepted my true self. It really stinks when we hide who we are. It was like being gay and finally coming out of the closet. You know that there's a whole society of people not willing to accept you. After all, what would my twelve years of Irish Catholic schooling say? Sister Patty Ann and Sister Assumpta would not be happy. (Or would they?) In my world, my psychic information highway comes from a very spiritual place, so maybe those nuns would be proud of me after all!

For several years I had the guilt thing happening and was careful not to tell too many people what I do for a living. But having three children in three years can really give you courage. That day in my kitchen, I found my authentic self as soon as I said those words; "I'm ready to do this psychic thing." I was crossing people over at night, telling souls to go into the light, seeing spirits in my house, feeding two babies, and entertaining a three years old, all while regaining the role I'd always had of helping the dead.

As with anything new, I had to study. I took a yearlong intensive course on all healing modalities. I worked with my psychic gift and had teachers from all over the world helping me to craft my work and discover WHO I was. I knew that I had better do this right, or I would have to contend with the negative image my industry has for the rest of my life, and again deal with being misunderstood.

Fourteen years later, I have a private practice, I'm a published author in a collaborative work, my show *Psychic Cup of Coffee* has been on the radio nationally and internationally for over three years now, and my own book is being published. All of this good came to be because one day while making baby formula, I took a chance on me and put my fear about other people's biases away, and became what I truly am; a psychic medium. I knew then that I had the talent to do this work.

I'm thrilled that I've grown up to be a medium. Today I use my gift and my voice to explain how this intuitive veil works within all of us. I'm able to be a teacher and assist people in understanding this authentic work with humility and humor. As a messenger of this work, I always present it from its "Highest and Best Intention." These are words that I live by and I recite them every day. No words should ever make you feel fear, especially coming from a psychic medium. If they do, walk out of the reading. You have a hooligan presenting. Your passed loved ones would be ticked off knowing that you're getting ripped off in a message. They view this information as a very holy hello from them, so find a qualified medium and don't get taken.

The prevailing image is that all psychics engage in meaningless "hocus pocus" as a money grab. There is certainly some truth to that stereotype, as there are bad apples posing as psychics, just as there are phonies in many other professions. There's also an important message here. Do not get overcharged. I had a client once tell me that they were charged six hundred and fifty dollars for a reading. Then they called me because they were so disappointed that this famous medium did not connect with them. For that kind of money, your passed loved one should have not only come through but made you dinner! Another scam I see in my line of work is famous mediums that have a media platform charging more for tickets in the front row, as if Spirit is going to come to you first because you've paid a hundred and fifty bucks for a ticket instead of fifty for general admission. Don't get taken by the losers in my profession who do this. It's just a shady way to take your money.

Overall, psychic mediums provide a valuable service in several industries, and to many people wishing to connect to their loved ones who have passed on. They work with a strong love vibration and are pretty holy people. They do this work for the love of it, despite the negative image it sometimes gets. I know this to be true because I am a psychic medium who really does care about people, and I have the privilege of working with many others who do too.

I would define myself as a Catholic, a Spiritualist, and a Buddhist, all wrapped into one. As a medium I get to experience daily that there is indeed such a thing as the afterlife. When I do a reading for a client, the messages come from a spiritual place that I can only describe as having the energy of holiness. If it came from a bad or evil place, I wouldn't touch it with a ten foot pole. Quite frankly, I'd be too scared.

To know that I'm able to provide comfort as a conduit for a mother who has lost a child, or for someone who has lost a parent, is an honor that I don't take lightly. My information comes from a very spiritual place which I can only describe as the energy of holiness. It's effective and still wows me every time I consult. The reactions I receive are overwhelmingly positive. People are often surprised by the messages I pass along to them and ask me "How did you know that?" during the course of the reading.

I woke up to a new assignment a few days ago while getting the kids off to school. It included twenty eight pages of information about college-aged men who had disappeared in Minnesota, dating back from 1999 to the present. These young men are either still missing or have been found in surrounding waterways. My job is to look at each case to see if there is more evidence that I can provide or to determine if there is a possible link among them. I'm volunteering part of my morning, while doing laundry, to work on this case.

I often work on these cases between loads of laundry and a few cups of coffee or a client or two. Then I gear up for the second shift in my house, which is picking up the kids from school and practice. I'm guided by Spirit and my intuition, working for the souls on the other side and attempting to provide closure for them. From what I understand from Spirit, all souls who have left this world in a traumatic way want to make it right. They want to give peace to their families that are left behind. Another soul layer revealed. Think about all those unsolved cases that show up twenty, thirty, or forty years later due to DNA evidence found, new clues, or confessions surrounding a case. Don't you know that's the soul helping out to make their story right? A murdered soul wants to expose the truth of what happened to cause their death, even if it is forty years later. They want closure for themselves and their loved ones left here on Earth.

My friend Tom Shamshak,from Shamshak Investigative Services, who works in the investigations of missing persons cases, has been quoted as saying "I think we owe it to our missing and dead, on behalf of our civilization, that we never cease our efforts to seek truth and seek justice" Well said Tom. The souls who are missing or have passed agree with you one hundred percent.

I wear many hats in my line of work as a psychic medium. The only one I don't wear is a witch's hat.

Now where did I leave my broom?

The   kitchen   floor   needs   to   be   swept...

CHAPTER 7   I AM A PSYCHIC DETECTIVE

I have surprised myself these past few years by becoming a psychic detective, work that picked me. I do it to find the missing and try to bring some peace to their families. Never did I ever think in a million years that I would dive into such a world but I did. Although my work can be draining and difficult, I do it for the souls who have been murdered or for people who are currently missing.

When someone disappears, that soul wants to be found in order to give closure to their death, life, and soul path. Their energy is in the category of "Don't screw with me." You've crossed the ultimate "soul line" when you kill someone. As a medium, I gather the information from a case that comes from the soul that's crossed, and I give it to the families of the victims, the police detectives, or the state agencies that request my work.

Even though I work with the families here, I'm really working with the victims from the other side. I represent them, and I'm a "shark" at obtaining the evidence because I'm compelled to make it right.

I'm tired of the total disregard for human life that criminals, rapists, child molesters, and evil people think they can get away with. Who gave them the right to do such injustice to humanity and the soul contract we all have as human beings? I have the attitude that "The buck stops here" when I get a case. The energy of the victim and the information that I receive is so powerful that it comes from a totally different place than when I consult for a normal reading. I can feel the shift when I read. It's so different than a normal psychic read. The energy changes and I start getting the information from a higher dimension. This is how I can tell if the person has passed, or has not crossed over and is just missing. When they have actually passed, the link is stronger.

If someone takes a life, be ready for the fallout from the soul's attitude. It'll kick your ass from here to China! My grandmother and mother always used to say "Fear the living not the dead." That saying is so true. People shouldn't fear psychic experiences or loved ones coming through to them. Fear the living, because some may try to do damage to you. Be cautious and protective of yourself, family, and friends. Think smart so as not to become a victim. Listen to your intuition when it says "Get the heck out of there!" I hope everyone learns to pay attention to those instincts. You should never, ever walk somewhere by yourself if it doesn't feel right. The buddy system you were taught in the first grade is still good advice when you're an adult.

I went to college at Western Michigan University in Kalamazoo, Michigan. I was a five-year plan girl, with a "C's get Degrees" attitude, and yes, I could throw a hell of a party. (Still can!) Anyway, on a Sunday evening during my senior year, (November 14th, 1987, to be exact) I was going to go for a run at a track on campus. At the last minute, as I was lacing up my sneakers, I heard a voice in my head saying "Don't go!!!" So I didn't. The next morning a girl named Julie Cunningham, a freshman from Vicksburg, Michigan, was found raped and strangled to death under the bleachers. That day she did the same thing I was going to do; just go out for an evening run. She was an innocent victim of being by herself in the wrong place at the wrong time.

The perpetrator, Timothy Bergman, acted like he had witnessed the slaying by telling the police details that they knew only the person who committed the crime would know. He was taken into custody November 24, 1987, and transferred to a psychiatric hospital. He had a history of mental illness and a prior rape conviction. His punishment for the rape and murder was life in prison without parole. Justice was served according to our judicial system, but was justice really served for the Cunningham family? The answer to that would be "NEVER."

That spring, in her honor, I became a student representative for a program called "Take Back the Night." It's a national program which hosts a candlelight vigil and a walk at night to protest violence against women, and to promote awareness about sexual assault and domestic violence.

To this day, over twenty- four years later, and often in Julie Cunningham's honor, this rally is still held. Her voice and message continue to live on, and her soul continues to work even though she's in Heaven. Souls on the other side feel honored when we remember them. No soul ever wants to be forgotten, especially when their physical death came about through murder.

Her spirit is also recognized by a scholarship given in her honor to a freshman from Vicksburg High School who's attending Western Michigan University. The scholarship offers a freshman twelve paid college credits per semester of their freshman year. Think of how many lives she and her family have touched. So there is good in this story. Not that any parent wants this type of "good" in their lives, but it's important to know that Julie's soul is touched every time a young person receives this scholarship. She grows right along with that person. I still pray for Julie Cunningham's soul to this day. I want her to be healed and to understand that her soul was never wasted. Her soul is blessed and alive, just in another dimension.

The choices you make in your daily life can keep you safe or make you vulnerable. If your psychic voice shouts at you, you darn well better listen! That Sunday evening I chose to listen to my inner knowing. If more people listened to their instinctual and psychic self, I would be out of business in my missing persons work and that would be fine with me.

The moral of this story is to always listen to your inner voice. When your intuition tells you something, please, please listen. It can sometimes be a big shout out like it was for me, or just a faint whisper. Regardless of how the information or "voice" is sent to you, please pay attention to its signs and symbols. It could very possibly save your life or prevent you from a horrible trauma. My inner guidance shouted at me that day. By the grace of God, I listened.

Sometimes cases will fall in my lap and sometimes I seek them out. Whatever the situation, we always find each other. This makes for a good partnership because I love this work. Remember, I work for the highest and best good intention. When I've had the opportunity to work with families and find evidence that provide closure, there's nothing better in this world. I always say it's like getting an Academy Award from Spirit for a job well done! I don't want to make light of this work. Trust me; it can be very heavy emotionally. I try to let go of evidence when I'm done but sometimes it sticks with me even when my boundaries are up. Even though we're psychic mediums, we're still human! Plus remember,

Spirit is always guiding us and wanting to solve their case, and sometimes they just don't let up. That's a fabulous thing. Connection is power and power can lead to closure and solving cases.

As I mentioned, I belong to several powerful groups with whom I do my psychic detective work. These groups are made up of psychic mediums, former FBI agents, private detectives, and police officers, who all put their heads together to solve cases. We have awesome energy, and as Tom Shamshack (who runs Boston University's Private Detective's Certification Program) says "Having a psychic on a case is like a case on steroids." That's a funny statement but very true. Psychics can have that affect. The information can just flow and flow. It's the detectives that then take the information and use it. We work on cold cases and go on site to find evidence and then give our humble opinions about what happened to these poor souls. It's the most difficult work you can do, which is why so many psychics shy away from it. That's fine too. We all have different gifts to be used in their own way. I have just chosen to use mine in this way. I didn't always do this type of work. I was asked to work my first case four years ago. I helped find the missing person and the details that I gave were one hundred percent spot on. This opened a new door in my work. Spirit will always shift you into what you should be doing as a medium. It constantly works with your vibration and changes it, which reveals another soul layer. This is how psychics evolve. Sometimes my evidence will come in through visions and then it will shift and come in through my hearing. Sometimes all of my senses are used. Our energy is used in ways that our physical body can handle depending on our own psychic energy field. It's kind of like tuning into a radio station. Spirit wants to find the right channel to work with. I trust the energy as to how it's to be revealed, and I also trust that I was picked to do this line of work.

Like everything in my life, I want to do it well, and I do.

Onto Some Cases:

Remember how I said that sometimes Spirit finds me? Well, one day I was in my kitchen working away. I like to cook so there's a good chance of finding this medium there! I kept seeing flashes of energy, and then I saw a small woman or teenager, dark hair and eyes, and very petite. In my world, I knew I was getting a heads up that I would be doing a reading.

Most mediums will tell you that Spirit shows up early sometimes, and when they do, it's important and they want your attention. That evening, my phone rang at 10:30 pm. The call was from someone asking me if I knew about their missing family member and saying that they had been referred to me by a client I had read months before. I told them that no, I hadn't heard about this, as they were in a different state than I was. I also said that I'd be happy to help, and that we could make an appointment for the next day. I got off the phone and thought "Why did I answer that call?" I never answer my work phone this late. Then I realized that their missing family member, a woman, was the Spirit I had seen in my kitchen. She had just shown up early for her appointment! I knew she had already passed on, and that she was getting my attention so I'd answer the phone and make the appointment.

I would be providing connections for her family, the Romaine's, for the next five months. I was able to give them the evidence as to where she would be found after three months, almost to the day, of the first reading.

At the time I was first connected with her family, Joann had been missing for a week. I described her as a small, petite girl/woman with dark hair and eyes. I thought at the time it was a young girl, but it was his sister, who was quite small. I was describing her uncles who were with her in Spirit. She was telling me she didn't commit suicide. She had strong Catholic beliefs and this would be the last thing she'd do. I knew this was the direction the investigation was taking and it was WRONG. I saw water. She was by water when she went missing. It was foul play. I saw two men abduct her and I knew she was murdered. It turned out she had been abducted at a church by the water, on a weekday night while going to attend mass. She told me "I was followed." I could feel her anxiety.

I worked with her daughter, who was just the most amazing child, and all of twenty- eight at the time. Her strength was the glue that kept her family together during this difficult time. Many details from her mother, of loss and anguish, flew out of me. Her mom's energy wanted to make it right, and that she did.

In January, I told Michelle, Joann's daughter, that her mom would be found in March. I kept seeing spring flowers and saw this as a sign that she would be found at that time. I told her she was northwest of an area called Bell Isle. I saw a bridge. I saw fishermen there. I saw a park that was nearby, and gave her the name. I knew she was in the water and I knew she would be found.

On March 21st, the second day of spring and, incidently, my birthday, Joann's body was found on the Canadian side of the bridge, northwest of the area I had targeted in my information. The fact that two fishermen had found her body, hooked on a fishing line, was no coincidence. I was told later that it was the line that had kept her body from washing out to the river. If that hadn't happened, her body would have never been found.

This was the best birthday present I could have gotten. I cried with relief and happiness knowing that her energy had lead me to the information that her family needed. There's truly nothing better. This case is still not closed. The investigation into her death continues. The perpetrator of this crime has not been caught...YET. This family keeps the investigation alive. They use the media every chance they get and work every single angle to try to ensure that justice is served. The media can be your best friend when people go missing. I'm always amazed when families shy away from it. It's the most misguided thing a family can do. If handled properly, the media can lead to clues to help your investigation. It's been four years since Joann's murder and the family has now put up billboards with an investigative hot line so people can call with information concerning the her death. They're not letting this case rest, nor is the woman on the other side: Joann Matouck Romaine.

I'm confident that justice will be served in this case. The energy of this homemaker and mother of three will make sure of it. It was with grace, and a desire for her dignity to be honored, that I was able to assist on this case. I always say "For grace is used in the power of the mystic." I believe it's by the "Grace of God" that I'm able to connect and do this work.

The right words from someone are always a gift, in any profession, and a thank you always makes you feel good.

Here's a thank you I got from Joann's family after working on her case. Remember that Academy Award feeling I have when I help solve a case? This is even better.

Kelle,

Words cannot even describe how grateful and thankful I am for finding you, and talking with you. You have the greatest gift that God could ever offer, and I feel so special and so blessed that you chose to share that gift with me and my family. I am so glad that you had that connection with my mom that you literally became her angel that she was able to speak through to reach out to us.

You have been so great through this tragedy, and honestly, without you, I don't know how I would have made it through... and I from the bottom of my heart thank you for your support. You have been great and deserve nothing but the best in this life. It's the least God can give you for being such a great person.

Love Always,

Michele.

I framed this and put it in my office to remind myself why I do this work. I really do have the most compassionate, best job in the world, and I thank God every day for the ability to do this work.

What Group Energy does: The Psychic Press Release

When you work in a group, the energy takes on a higher level. It flows. It's sent at the highest vibration and the information is sent completely unclouded and clear. It all becomes ONE. When our groups get together, like the Cold Case Collaborative or Find Me, the information becomes more consistent between the people involved. When we're given a case, the only information we get is the name of the missing, the date they went missing, where they went missing, and their birthday. As psychic mediums, we are to provide the "who, what, when, where, and how" to the case. It's often like doing a psychic press release. We answer those questions and deliver the information. When we work, we first work individually, and then the information gets collaborated by the group. It's then sent off to the proper authorities.

It always amazes me how very similar our information is when we compare it. I get my information by hearing it, feeling it, and seeing it. For example, I may say "perp has black hair, mustache, and tattoo on right arm. Body will be found under woodpile, power lines by body, etc…" My fellow medium friend and caseworker, Nancy Smith, is a Spirit artist. She sketches what she sees in relation to a case and draws what I hear, see and feel. I've also seen that when two Spirit artists work a case, their sketches will end up looking the same. See how the information is given and how it's provided through mediums in a variety of ways? No one works the same. The consistency in detail, even given the different ways we pick up the facts, is amazing to me. I'm always floored by how the evidence shows up.

Here's an example of how a cold case collaborative worked a case:

In October of 2007, Charlie Allen was a young college student missing from Dartmouth College, in Massachusetts. His story was featured on a show called *Psychic Kids*. Chris Flemming, (psychic medium) Chip Coffey, (psychic) and Tom Shamshack, (brought in as a private investigator) as well as several teenagers with psychic ability, worked this case for the TV program.

We, as a group, took it on. A few years later, our information was shown to be consistent with what they found while taping. No surprise there. Chris Fleming had done an EVP (electronic voice phenomenon) recording to see if there was any evidence of a voice in the area he was in. Before I got the EVP recording, I dove into my Psychic Press Release and my information consisted of the following:

- Brian- name connected to the case.
- Heard the words "Help Me." These words were heard on the EVP recording when I listened later.
- Saw small pills in a pocket - drugs.
- He showed me walking upstairs in a house. He was upstairs in a house he didn't know.
- Mary/Margaret - family connection to him.
- He lived with others on campus, not traditional living. He hated where he lived.
- Good marks, good at manipulating situations.
- He told me in this case, he was manipulated.

How did he pass away?

- Head trauma, violent act, destructive imagery around his death, drug connection to his death, money dealings, feeling chased, being hunted.
- Dumped in wooded area behind a stump.
- He wore a bracelet, sailor's knot, white. Remember for evidence.
- The number seven is consistent with case.
- Seven miles outside of campus.
- Saw a Wal-Mart.
- Insignia on bridge.
- Bi-polar mental illness. In a different house.

So here are the facts to the Charlie Allen Case:

- His car was found in lot 7. He slept in his car.
- 271 Slocum Road was where his backpack was found.
- 7 College Lane is where he was last seen in the upstairs of the house.
- He was disorientated and went into someone's house. He jumped from the upstairs bedroom, barefoot, and ran.

- Owner of the house called police to report a break in.
- Shoes found on Schoolhouse Lane.

This was one of the largest searches for a missing person ever conducted in the state of Massachusetts. When the CCC from the Boston University went together to the site, we ended up on Woodbury Lane, not knowing that this was an area where *Psychic Kids* had filmed the show. Automatically, everyone was drawn to this area, also not knowing that this was the location where the police dogs had lost his scent.

Prior to the location outing, I had sat in Spirit, looking for clues and information. Now remember, mediums often get random information. I kept seeing a gun and I remember thinking, "Oh crap! Am I going to get shot when I go to Dartmouth?" When we started walking in this area, I heard gunshots. The gunshots were coming from a gun club up the road. This was evidence to me that my guides were pointing me in the right direction. While walking, I looked down and saw the rope, similar to a sailor's knot. I know this was more evidence to me that my guides were directing me to the right spot.

Nancy couldn't attend, but drew what she got from Spirit from her home. Her drawings are often like psychic treasure maps. They'll have clues of things to look for. Now remember, things sometimes come in symbolically. In this case, she drew an octagonal shape. As we walked into the forested area, to the right of the entrance we saw an octagonal picnic table. These are just a few examples of what we were given about the case.

As our group concluded our gathering, we compiled our data and sent it to the proper authorities in the hope that it could assist in the case. Unfortunately, to date the case is still unsolved.

It really, really, bugs me when cases go unsolved. I've always believed that it would be very beneficial if police detectives worked with a psychic partner too. Imagine all the information that could be verified. I get the fact that this information can't be used in court, but who cares? The information that I can provide is just a tool to be used, something extra that the police can research to see if it helps.

What's wrong with that? I can't think of a thing. Some detectives welcome the information but others don't. For the old, crusty egos in the police department who don't believe in psychics, I have news for ya; you're pretty intuitive yourself. You wouldn't have picked this line of work unless you had psychic ability. So, to put it bluntly, why would you "poo-poo" a field that you're just as much a part of?

I view these roles as similar to the ones that were in play when I sold real estate. Everyone had a role in the transaction. As the agent, I sold the house and arranged for the buyers to sign a purchase and sales agreement. Then the attorney took over. You passed the baton onto the next player, just as you do during a psychic investigation. My role is to work with the soul. The police take the information and research it and match the information against their facts.

Would I love to be onsite with cases, be a part of an investigation early on? You betcha! You know why? Because time and money are resources that the missing desperately need. The best way to ensure that these resources will be available is to find the person responsible for their disappearance as soon as possible. When you fast forward six months, one year, or five years, the case is cold. The attention, the money, and the resources are dead, just like many of the missing.

The money and manpower that used to fuel state and national investigations aren't there anymore. Since 9/11, our monies are sent to protect our borders. Our resources are tapped, there's no follow through on cases like there used to be, so they can't be solved. Some cities' success rates in the solving of murder cases are down over thirty percent. It's a big problem for our cities.

How sad is this? How would you like to be that mom, dad, daughter, or son, left not knowing what happened to a child or parent? Even worse, how many more times has that "perp" been free to kill again?

So my problem with those old, crusty attitudes in agencies that say "We got this," or "I don't need a psychic's help," is that it's just not true. You don't "got this." Your case is at a dead end so it's doomed to become another cold case. Your ego's too involved. Step back and let some fresh energy take a look and assist you with your case. You and your ego can take the credit for cracking it. Who cares? I sure don't. All the soul wants is for their case to be solved.

I'm fine with that. Remember, I work for the souls on the other side. They don't care about ego. Their energy comes from love. They give me, the conduit, important information to be passed on in order to make things right. They never, ever say "We got this" and blow me off.

How Spirit Thanked Me

The biggest thank you I ever got from Spirit was in July of 2011, while working a case about a young girl missing in New Hampshire. I was asked to work on this case by two of my colleagues. There was such urgency to this case because I really felt that this eleven year old little girl was still alive when I was reading on it. Her name was Celina Cass. Normally when we work, we collaborate and then send the information to the police agencies. I couldn't wait, so I told everyone to do it separately and we'd send it in together later on.

Soon after, all of our information was off to the FBI command post. On July 30, 2011, I knew if she was not found within five days that she would be dead. On August 4th, on the way to my office where we were meeting as a group, I got a phone call from an investigator who told me that a body had been found in a dam, a few miles from her home.

My intuition, my mediumship, was still filling me with a continued sense of urgency to find her alive. I knew this child was not dead when I read the first time. I didn't have that shift I normally feel when someone has passed while I'm working on their case. Unfortunately, it was indeed the young girl we so wanted to find alive.

My two Spirit artists had drawn pictures of the perpetrator, and even though they hadn't been together, the pictures looked very much alike. Our notes were all similar as well.

Three months after this case, I went for a reading of my own. Yes, once in a blue moon, I have a reading done. People think a psychic should be able to read herself, but it doesn't work that way; another revelation of how the psychic soul works. I'm pretty good at listening to my intuition and guides, but I never read myself. It's just not good practice. Too close to home, I guess. So off I went to Maine to see this psychic medium that I had waited a year to see, named Judy Turner.

I arrived and we sat down to do my reading and connect. She gave me information about my work life. She obviously knew what I did. My loved ones who had passed on were coming through. And then she came upon a little girl. She started describing her to me and I started to cry. She was describing the child from the investigation. Judy was giving the exact evidence I had been given on the case. She could have never known these details. (See? Even I am impressed with how Spirit works!)

This beautiful child linked to me and thanked me for helping her and asked me to keep working on her case. I was awestruck and I couldn't talk; a first for me. I was filled with such emotion. Spirit, a soul, had come back to thank me! For me, this was just amazing.

I really knew in that moment that I was on the right path. I would continue to volunteer my time, and I would always assist souls on the other side to make right their anguish and loss.

The anniversary of this child's death is coming up. I have resent my information to the authorities and gotten the usual "We got this." (Oh, really?) I will continue working to find the missing link and to get my information about this little girl's case heard.

No sooner did I finish that last paragraph when my husband called me at my office. "Kelle, call this detective. He's left three messages for you." I'm very fortunate to have found a person in the investigation to hand off our information too, again in the hope that our information can assist this beautiful child get her closure. See how the connection of Spirit works? It always humbles me.

My prediction is that the coming years will be years of illumination. You'll be seeing a lot of old cases being solved. Why do I say this? Because our energy, and the energy of the other side's guides and loved ones, has changed. The intuitive link between Spirit and the living is ramping up in preparation for the coming years. You can be sure that psychics will be used to solve a lot of cases. If I were a police detective, I'd be taking out all those old cases and reviewing them. I'd be giving them the once over, because suddenly the clues will be found. I'd be calling in psychic detectives to give these cases a whirl and to see what their intuition could find. This is how strongly intuition will be used, by all of us, in the near future. So detectives, get ready for a lot of good work to be done, because new information will be flooding your offices. A good example of this is the recent Cleveland case where three missing girls were found alive. They had been kept captive for ten years by their kidnapper. It gave everyone reasons for renewed hope. It also opened the eyes of many police agencies and compelled them to take a closer look at their cold case files.

The veil is no longer a veil. Think about the word "illumination" and what it represents. According to the good ole' Webster Dictionary it means: "To enlighten spiritually and/or intellectually." Based on that definition, I predict that many "hopeless" cases will finally be solved. And not a moment too soon for the families still holding their breath and waiting for news.

CHAPTER 8 DEATH AND MY EXPERIENCE

So what does this psychic medium think of death? What happens to the soul? Where do we go? Will they serve hot fudge sundaes, or will we have to diet in heaven? These are some of the questions I have actually answered when I've been asked about death. The last few are pretty funny, but I believe that the holy energy we enter when we die is just more of life, sprinkled with some wholeness and peace. It really is kind of like a sundae, and who doesn't like ice cream?

If the energy dictates that you show yourself as a size eight, hot looking woman, then that's your choice. You will no longer have to be the fat, eighty year old lady with wrinkles that you were when you died.

I have seen that Spirit can show themselves at any age they choose. When loved ones come through in a reading, they can show up as they were at any point in their lives. Any psychic can say during a read "I have an old woman with white hair coming through," which is way too generic. If the Spirit describes herself to me as she would have looked in her thirties, (by her clothing type, hairstyle, etc…) that is Spirit making the choice as to how they want to be presented. This is just another way that Spirit manifests. A soul directs their information as to how they want to be revealed. They have the power of choice just like we do. I'm always amazed by the evidence they pick. Sometimes they appear as they were during the best time of their life. Trust me when I say there are plenty of sixties' style bouffant hairdos showing up in readings! Men are showing up in the suits and hats that they wore in the forties and fifties. The fashion details work with their personalities. It could be the farmer in his overalls with a red kerchief in his back pocket or a dancer in her tutu. Bottom line is, whatever Spirit chooses to give as evidence will be what's best remembered by the client, and often represents the Earth time that they had enjoyed the most. This translates to me that Heaven is a very happy place. You get to pick the era you want to be in, and how you look. You have a choice about how you show yourself for a reading!

The other side is simplified for souls. Things aren't chaotic like they are here. It's whole energy, the energy we have not explored yet. It's the feeling of knowing when your gut instinct is right, but twenty times over with awesomeness! What the other side is like is a constant wonder for human beings everywhere. I can answer these questions about Heaven from my own experience when I'm connecting. It's simply love, freedom, and contentment within oneself.

A client once told me a story about an experience she had after her husband had passed. He had come through to her while she was driving, her hand hanging out the window on a beautiful day. He said to her "This is what it feels like where I am." What a wonderful message! I've heard Spirit say things like "It's just great here," or "It's so much love." My interpretation is that the vibration is so strong that it feels really fast. It probably isn't, but that's how it feels to Spirit. When we drive, the speed limit is usually 65mph on the highway, but on the other side they drive 110mph, and that's O.K! Can you imagine? I'm a "10 and 2" driver. (Remember driver's Ed?) I can't even imagine my energy being so fast. I do understand however, how high their energy level is when we connect. I guess I can be a fast driver! Vibrationally, they move much faster than we do and that's their normal. I've never, ever done a reading where I've had a negative, ugly interpretation of where their energy was coming from. And that goes for people who committed suicide as well.

My interpretation of what happens to a person that takes their own life is that sometimes they just can't hack it here. They need the enlightenment of God to help them through whatever difficult task their soul has picked to deal with here on earth. Remember too, that their soul may have already gotten the answers as to why they came, and they needed to leave quickly. They may have needed the assistance of passed loved ones, parents, grandmothers, grandfathers, or some other guide to help them. Maybe mere humans just couldn't do for them what they needed to have done, and you know what? That's O.K. All souls have lessons, both here and there. Eventually they'll understand what they need, and move on within to another soul reveal. They're doing just fine and their soul is growing. I promise you, they're resolving their pain with so much love and understanding. It's the true love vibration that heals them at this time.   Some of the hardest readings emotionally are from suicide victims. There are so many unanswered questions for the families left behind. Why, Why, and... Why?   They'll tell my clients how sorry they are that they've caused such grief by leaving so quickly and under such stressful circumstances. They'll give messages of comfort, love, and deeply felt regret for the choice they had to make. They want to balance the injustice they've done. They will be healed and whole again, as we all will be someday. Please don't think that these souls are in purgatory or are being punished in some way. It's quite the opposite. They're surrounded by LOVE to help them understand their life/soul choice.

Who wins in this situation? Not the people left behind, that's for sure. But the person who died gets the healing of empowerment from the other side so that they can transform. There also may be some lessons the loved ones that were left here on Earth needed to get. There are always concrete lessons within any tragedy.   Life is always about growth, wherever you are.   There's a strong, heartfelt, loving message for everyone when the soul's choice is suicide. The anguish can be unbearable, but we need to know that our loved one's soul made a choice, and that that choice was just the lesson they needed to get. They're immersed in pure love and light to assist in their healing. They are being healed. Understanding these messages can sooth the hurt and grief that's felt by the family left behind.

I did a reading for a lovely woman who had seen an article I had written for our local paper. Her son had committed suicide the year before and the anniversary was coming up. Ryan, her son, came through with all kinds of love and evidence for his mom. It was a beautiful and touching reading. One month later, in December, I got this note in the mail:

Dear Kelle,

I am writing today to thank you again for the reading you did with me on the phone on Nov 16th. I also wanted to send you a copy of a poem that our son Ryan wrote at age 15.

The reading with you was very helpful and comforting to me in regards to Ryan's suicide. It is hard enough to lose a child, but it is even worse to not know what happened.

You mentioned you were writing a book, and I will be looking for that to be published.

Again, my sincere thanks to you and your amazing insight and talent.

Merry Christmas from me to you and your family.

Lynne

Ryan's Poem written to his mom on Valentine's Day:

Hearts give us life,
hearts give us love.
Hearts give us grace,
like the sweet morning dove.

Hearts give us feelings,
either sad or good.
Hearts would give us freedom,
if they could.

Hearts see our future,
hearts saw our past.
If hearts could cure,
they'd do it real fast.

Hearts produce miracles,
I guess you could say.
Hearts are always working, especially on V-day.

By Ryan Meagher

This young man has an empowering message for all of us, doesn't he? He didn't need eighty years to grow his soul here on Earth. He left his message early on with the enlightened words he used in his poem. How blessed are we to have just read such beautiful, kind words? Ryan found his grace at age fifteen and continues to have it today, but now, it's in Spirit.

We all feel anguish when we have to let a loved one go. Our link to them is so strong and valued it can become a deep sorrow for us. Some days it hits us physically and rocks us to our core. A core we didn't even know existed.

We are all resilient. God has made us tough cookies. Most of us do accept the grief at some point, but we still need to work through it in stages. We hate the process, but we do it. There's always a piece of us that holds a little sadness. This is completely normal. At some point though, we do learn a new normal without our loved ones, and sometimes that's just the best we can do.

Spirit wants us to have our new normal. They want our days to be beautiful and filled with goodness and love. They don't want tears shed over them. They want jokes and laughter and lightheartedness in memory of who they were. Yep, they know that you're hurting; they sure do. But I believe they want to help us heal. I've seen this through the evidence they show me. We've all seen them and felt their signs, whether through dreams or circumstantial evidence. The other side makes sure of it. They have the energy to do it through a funny saying, a song played, a light flickered, or a penny found. Whatever the symbol, they'll be sure to send it to you at the right time to comfort you. You have all received your own evidence from them, whether you recognized it or not. And you didn't even need a medium to show you. Imagine that!

Spirit is great at showing themselves, so welcome the evidence into your life. Those little signs are not coincidences. They're all planned. I always say that the other side's agendas and iPhones are much better than ours. The data is ready to be sent to you in an instant. Be open and ready to receive it.

My Experience with Death

When my father, Ritchie Teets, was diagnosed with Stage 4 melanoma cancer, he was told by his doctors to get his affairs in order. It was pretty much a cut and dry case of cancer caught too late. The cancer had attacked his lungs and was starting to take whatever organ it damn well wanted. My immediate family all lived in Michigan. I was the only sibling living elsewhere. One of the worst things to contend with was not being there when I wanted to be, but I would come and go as often as I could. At that time I had children that were eight, six, and five years old, had just moved to a new town, owned two houses, (one of which I was trying to sell) and had a husband working ninety hours a week at a high tech startup company. Could my life have been any more stressful and complicated? There are days now when I look back and don't even know how I swam through all that stress. But I managed a backstroke or two to survive it, because I had too.

Spirit guided me when I needed it most,
as it always does.

In July, my dad was told he was dying. We were all there. His kidneys were shutting down, he was being given last rites, and his body was physically failing him, but he didn't die. We loved him back to life and he rallied with us until September. During those cherished extra months my father gave us a gift; to be a part of the process of his death. During those months we would have twenty, sometimes thirty people coming over for dinner every night. Each time, someone would bring a meal to share. They would come to pay homage and give big love to my dad Ritchie.

It was amazing to watch. I swear my dad stuck around longer just for the fun of it. The party was too good to leave. That was so true to his personality. There were plenty of times growing up when he would be the last one out the door, singing with my Uncle Jimmy "Show me the way to go home, I'm tired and I wanna go to bed! I had a little drink about an hour ago and it went straight to my head"…some forties song. My dad was fun. He was always the first one out on a dance floor and he just loved everyone he met. I hope this gives you a small glimpse into who he was.

My Father was also the patriarch of his family, coming from a brood of eight brothers and sisters. He was truly the "salt of the Earth." He loved the game of golf and really enjoyed all the people he met while on the golf course. That was as important to him as the game itself. People loved my dad because he loved people. He really never did meet a stranger.

So many people never get to say goodbye to their loved ones. Some of the hardest readings are when grief lingers, often for a lifetime. I have seventy year old men coming for readings, trying to resolve the pain of not having been able to say good bye or get that last "I love you." They've been holding onto this grief for twenty years or more all because they feel they didn't get to properly let go of the final link to their loved one's humanity, giving them soul closure. I'm a big proponent of letting people say their last goodbyes whenever they can, and that includes children. You're not helping them by shielding them from the process of death. The person dying is a part of them, just as they're a part of you. They're linked to that person just as much as you are. As parents, one should never deny them that privilege. They too own the death experience. Parents often, out of love, have the misguided belief that they're protecting them because they themselves find death painful. It can leave them with a lifetime of pain if you make the wrong choice. And guess what? The person that's dying may need that last "I love you" from a beloved child to give them permission to lift off to the beautiful place that they're leaving us for. Always treat death with respect, not shame or fear. We treat birth with grace and dignity. We should treat death with the same respect. It's a learning opportunity, a healing event, and you will be thankful one day to have witnessed it. The soul wants you to know that death is nothing to fear.

My family's gift was getting closure from a man that taught us many lessons in life. In his last months of living, we were given the gift of process. Make no mistake; death is a process, just like birth. This is true even for those that die in the blink of an eye. It may have been a few minutes rather than a month, but there was still a process for their soul as they transitioned. But have no fear, the end result is and always will be beautiful.

In my opinion, it's easier for family and friends to grieve when the death of a loved one is more gradual. I see it in my practice every day. The most important thing that Spirit wants you to know is that how they lived, not how they died, is what matters. We tend to feel the need to dwell on the details of death. Spirit, on the other hand, feels that death itself is rather unimportant. They would rather have their journey on Earth remembered. They understand that life is a journey and that we're lucky to have it. That's the message from Spirit.

I arrived home a few days before my father passed. Just as he had always shown up for the great events in my life, I wouldn't have missed his transition into his new world for anything. I was there to cheer him on along with the rest of my family. By this late stage, his body was pretty much ravaged by disease. If you've ever had to deal with cancer, you will certainly agree that it just sucks.

When I walked into my dad's bedroom after I had arrived from Boston, I remember saying "Dad, I'm here." I saw his whole face relax, and he smiled and said "Thanks Kel."

As the days went on I could see his life force becoming depleted. Then energetically I started to see a silver and gold light appearing, bright and glistening. It was something I'd never seen before. I often see aura colors when I read people, but this was different. I knew it was a sign of his soul preparing to release from his physical body. I would work his energy from his feet all the way to his head, releasing cords and sending healing for his transition, assisting and comforting his energy field. I just did anything I could to help him. We all did.

I remember that for days, I would see people he had loved who had passed before him. I even remember describing a man I didn't know, and my brother Ritchie said he was a person Dad had worked with. My brother and dad worked in the same industry, so he would have known this. I saw his parents and his brothers and sisters, who had also passed.

It confirmed for me once again that as my readings show, passed loved ones show up to help us cross into our next dimension; another soul revelation. They comfort our souls with love and recognition to help us release. Not one person passes alone. Their "helpers" are there to welcome them into this new dimension. I remember my dad telling my mom that he was not afraid to die. He would tell her "Just think of all the people I'm going to see again Marilyn." What a positive attitude he had. It wasn't fear based at all. It was based on an awareness of wholeness, don't you think? Now knowing how I described my father's life and how he led it, never meeting a stranger and being able to talk to anyone, can't you just imagine his own team of "helpers" waiting for him with open arms? When my father was passing, not only were all his loved ones with him in a twelve foot by fourteen foot bedroom, but the whole room was filled with Spirit. It was a little tight in there, but we all managed to fit!

My Father died at 5:30 am on September 23, 2005. Everyone he loved was there with him. One of the last things I saw energetically was this sliver cord releasing from his solar plexus, (belly area) then poof, it was gone! I knew his soul was on its journey and boy oh boy, what a ride it was going to be! My father needed us to aid him in his transition, and it was a blessing to all of us. That's how he wanted it, and so did we. My family learned so much from him, even in the last few days we spent with him.   What a wonderful, honest gift from a beautiful man.

I always tell my clients that whoever is supposed to be there when someone dies is who will be there.   How many times do you hear stories of families vigilantly watching over someone at their bedside, and the minute they get up to go to the bathroom or get a bite to eat their loved one dies? That's because sometimes our own vibration holds them back from transition. Love is very powerful.   It's a vibration that is so much more powerful than any other.   It's the purest of all emotions.

If you weren't there, it's O.K. It's what their soul needed to release. It was the soul's plan, that's all. Don't dwell on it. Your loved ones know you were there. They know you love them and that they were not alone, ever, at any moment. Their team of loved ones who had passed before them were holding their hand all the way, even if you weren't there to do it. Please understand that they were comforted.

Once your loved ones have crossed, keep your senses aware.   Look for those signs and symbols that are given right away. You need to ask for signs from your loved ones, you need to pay attention to your dreams, and you need to pay attention to the play of words that are used around you. These are all forms of energy that are here to assist you in getting confirmation from your loved ones that they're O.K and still with you. Let me share with you what I saw after my dad passed on.

My husband and kids flew in a day after he died, for the wake. One of the events we did at the funeral was to have all the grandchildren write messages and put the messages in balloons for a balloon release. The kids were sitting at the table writing their messages. (I would have loved to have been able to read them all!) My son Matthew, who was eight at the time, asked "What were Papa's last words?" Avery, who was six, said "Don't you know Matt? They were 'I love you all.' " Those were her grandfather's actual last words to us. Avery could have never known this as she was nine hundred miles away when my father died. Kids are so open and are clear channels for information from passed loved ones. Pay attention to those little ones for messages. Avery, the intuitive, had very naturally given her first message from Spirit, not even knowing the gift she had just given me. We then went to the cemetery to make the arrangements. There at the cemetery was my father's car, which he had sold two weeks before he died. It was a Buick Century nicknamed "La Bamba." (Like the song, because there were so many golf balls rolling around in the trunk that the car had its own beat.) There it was, "La Bamba," the same color, design, and year. "La Bamba had arrived, yet another sign. We proceeded to see that car for weeks, months, and years after he died. When I got back to Massachusetts, I saw the same car six times in a week. It was a symbol my family would see forever. Now when I see it, I always say "Hi Dad!" The grandkids say, "There's Papa's car!" When we pulled out of the cemetery, I looked up and saw Rich's Gas Station, my father's name.

All that symbolism, and all within 48 hours of his death, was a sign letting me know that he was just fine. As difficult as grief can be, it helps to see evidence from our loved ones that they're at peace and safe, and trust me, they really are. We're the ones that may not be doing so great. Nothing's coincidental. It's all confirmation that the message is from them. Our loved ones are in a good and healing space. They're happy and being honored in the place they now reside. They send us those messages to help us understand that they are well, and that you'll eventually be O.K. without them too. You'll find a new normal in your life without them, and someday your grief will be less raw.

I like to think those messages I got after my dad died, and the ones you'll get from passed loved ones, are like a wink from the other side. They're just checking in to let you know that all is well. Open yourself up to those winks that you get from Spirit. Your loved ones sure are giving them. You must pay attention to them so they're not missed. Those messages are reminders from your passed loved ones that they're still linked to you through the love that you shared in this lifetime. They honor you every day with little signs, so stay aware and look out for them … Wink! Wink!

My father and I last picture together.
Look at the Spirit Orbs in this photo.

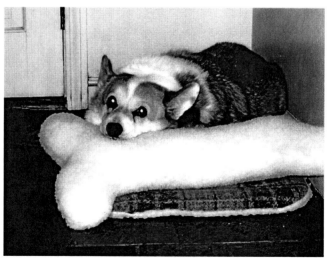

Kayleigh Dog-Hanging out in her "Corgi Corner",
right before she passed.

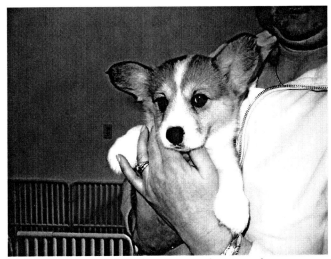

Kayleigh being true to her word:
sent us our new puppy *Maxine*!

My "Rocks" in County Kildare, Ireland,
feeding my psychic soul.

Boston Marathon April 15ᵗʰ 2013, room 911
on Antigua Island.

2 mediums from across the pond:
Bridget Benson & myself.

My grandparents *Grace & Harley Sloan.*
My intuitive grandmother communicated with me at
age 9…and that was my first message!

Kelle as a young school girl in her *"Good Shepherd"*
uniform, when my psychic experiences began.

NIKOLA TESLA CHILLIN' IN HIS LAB.

"If you wish to understand the Universe, think of energy, frequency, and vibration."

-Nikola Tesla

My man Nikola Tesla had a lot of vision when it came to electrical current and how energy works. I can relate to him. Although I haven't a clue as to how energy works from a scientific point of view, I do understand that we're all made of energy and that it's the frequency of our lives. From a psychic medium's perspective, it's everything. Our thinking towards ourselves and our lives and goals, as well as how we connect to everything is through our ENERGY. Although science sometimes has a hard time proving my work as a psychic medium, (they always try) I would be hard pressed not to say that I believe every inventor or scientist, such as Mr. Tesla, has visions, intuitions, or plain old fashioned gut instincts about their work, and that they always use the intuitive side of their brains.

Tesla often had visions of his work with electricity and how to create power. Back in the day, in the nineteen hundreds, they called him a visionary. He was way ahead of other people in his field. I'd like to call him a psychic.

He trusted his visions and acted upon them, and was thus able to transform our world. He developed electric generators, motors, and transformers. His insights still affect the way we live today. Tesla's greatest achievement is his polyphase alternating current system, which is used to this day to light up the entire globe.

He was also known for his many experiments that lead to innovation. He often had psychic visions. For instance, he knew when his parents would die. He had electrical visions that were given to him by intuition. With a flash of blinding light, they led him to his magnificent discoveries in science. He once said *"The desire that guides me in all I do is the desire to harness the forces of nature to service mankind."* I think that was a pretty noble ambition. What do you think?

I had the weirdest dream on May 28th, 2011. In my dream there was a man visiting me. He was really handsome, deep set eyes, and dark hair. His suit was an older style, so I knew that he was from another time. I felt connected to him but I didn't know how. He just felt familiar. Remember how I've said that there are always people in my dreams that I don't know? It didn't frighten me. It's happened before, but this was a little different. This was a visitation.

At the time, I didn't know what it meant. A few days later, I would come to understand what it was all about. But that morning I just woke up and thought "What a cool dream! Whoever that was, he sure was handsome!"

On June 1, 2011, I was off to New York to attend the Book Expo with my friend Nancy Smith. She had just written a children's book, and I was working on this book, so we went in hopes of understand the publishing world a little better. We jumped at the opportunity to attend one of the largest book expos in the world. We had to make last minute reservations though, and found ourselves at The New Yorker Hotel. When we checked in there was only one room left for early check in, so we grabbed it.

When we arrived at the room, there was a gold plaque on the door saying that this was Nikola Tesla's room. It said he had lived there for 10 years and it had a picture of him, along with a list of all of his accomplishments in power and energy.

I have to admit, at that time I had no idea who Nikola Tesla was. I graduated with a communication public relations degree and as my family will tell you, I'm far from technical. When I saw his picture, I thought "That man looks familiar and so handsome! Mmmm... how do I know this guy?" Suddenly, I knew that this man, Nikola Tesla, was the man who had visited me in my dream! Spirit often shows up early, and Mr. Tesla had made his presence well known to me before I was going to stay in his room. The room number was 3327. I was glad because I like numbers with the number three in them. My birthday is 3-21. In numerology, that is a 33 number. We were also on the 33rd floor, which also resonated with me.

He also was quoted as saying "If only you knew the magnificence of three, six, and nine, then you would have a key to the universe." He did everything in his life by these numbers. A little OCD, but it worked for him. He would walk around a block three times before entering a building. He worked from 9 am to 6 pm daily, and would resume his work at 3 am every night. Yep, threes were his thing.

I said to Nancy when I saw the plaque on the hotel room door, "This guy worked with energy and so do we, just a different kind!" We laughed, and then I said "How much sleep are we going to get tonight?" What are the odds of two mediums checking into a hotel and getting the last room available, and then it turns out to be Nicola Tesla's room? I think it was definitely meant to be. I also thought "No wonder it was the last room left. It's haunted by Mr. Tesla himself!"

This is a daily kind of occurrence in my world, but it can happen to you too if you stay open and welcome the information from the other side. They're always more than willing to communicate and check in. Just remember though, you'll only have that that type of visit if YOU want it.

Like I said, I knew nothing of Mr. Tesla's achievements. That night while talking to my husband I said "Hey have you ever heard of this guy Nikola Tesla? We're staying in the room that he lived in for ten years." Tom would know of Mr. Tesla because he's the Director of Engineering for a major computer company. He responded "Yeah, I know of him. He was the engineer behind the power of electrical energy, etc…" As Tom was speaking with me, he was googling his name and asked me what hotel we were staying in. I told him we were at The New Yorker. He said "It says here that not only had he lived at The New Yorker but that he actually died in room 3327 there." I gasped and whispered "We're *in* room 3327." Perfect.

I told Nancy, "No sleep for us tonight." During our stay we could feel his energy. Not bad or heavy, just hanging around. I had the feeling he was kind of reclusive and kept to himself in later years and Nancy agreed. She was also seeing lost papers, and documents everywhere.

I got the feeling that women wanted him and thought him to be mysterious. It turns out he was single his whole life. He kept women at bay most of the time; a "married to science" kind of thing. He was alluring to the people around him though. He was charming, but he puzzled people because he was complicated and obsessive.

At 3:33 am (Notice the numbers?) I was dog tired, but obviously Mr. Tesla was wide awake. This is the time he would start his day according to my research. Remember that the veil to the other side is thinnest at this time. This was the same time of night I had my last visitation from him. Spirit often shows up between one and four in the morning because it's quiet, making it easier for them to connect. We also have psychic experiences when we sleep. I was so tired, having been up at four in the morning the day before to travel to New York, and then spending all day at the trade show. I rolled over and wouldn't let him come through to me. (I know, I know, bad medium.)

Nancy on the other hand, tossed and turned all night, and at one point was playing solitaire on her phone. As she was playing the game, the phone started playing solitaire for her! Mr. Tesla's energy was joining in! The next morning when she told me the story, we both cracked up and I said "Why wouldn't he be playing solitaire on your iPhone? He would have loved the technology!" After all, didn't he create the concept of wireless electricity to make our world function as it does?

It looks to me like Mr. Tesla was way ahead of his time. His "enlightened visions" were actually future psychic predictions about technology and how our world could benefit from it.

According to Life Magazine in a special issue from September 1977, Tesla is among the one hundred most famous people of the last thousand years. And I spent the night with him! And not just once, but twice! He's still using his energy, just from the other side. He showed up when two mediums stayed in "his" room, room 3327, on the 33rd floor of The New Yorker Hotel.

Nikola Tesla was found dead on January 7, 1943, by a maid wanting to clean his room. She ignored the "Do Not Disturb" sign after two days and walked in to find his corpse. My intuition tells me he died on January 6, 1943, not on the seventh when he was found. For two days no one entered his room due to the "Do Not Disturb" sign left on the door.

In numerology, his birth date July 10, 1856, equates to the number nine year. His last day here on Earth was January 6, 1943, which would equal the number six. Both a nine and a six can be divided by three. He managed to follow the important numbers that ruled his life up to the very day he died. Not that surprising really.

After all, wasn't this the theory of his life? I'm sure he was happy with the timing of his death and wouldn't have had it any other way.

Nikola Tesla knew the importance of "grounding" in more ways than just what was covered by the technical definition.

"Everyone should consider his body as a priceless gift from one whom he loves above all, a marvelous work of art, of indescribable beauty, and mystery beyond human conception, and so delicate that a word, a breath, a look, nay, a thought may injure it."

Nikola Tesla
The Century Magazine, June, 1900

Readings from Spirit

This chapter was the most difficult for me to write. I've been reading for a long time, and to pinpoint what read would show the most evidence as an example of how Spirit works was very difficult for me. The readings all have their own message, and are all special in their own right. It's like trying to pick a best friend; you just can't. (Or at least I can't.) Sometimes all your friends are best friends!

Spirit always wants to "make good" with their loved ones. We're all part of the infinite. We're all a continuous link to the spiritual side of life. Our Spirit continues on, and that continuity of life is proven through mediumship.

Loved ones bring us divine inspiration through their humor, quirky ways, physical looks, and the signs and symbols that only YOU would understand. Why? It's because they're still with you. They're just linked to you from a higher side of love, that's all.

When our two worlds work together, we create harmony for the soul that has passed. It's often through a reading that the doorway to the other side is opened, and evidence of the soul is provided. Passed loved ones want to show you that they're with you. It's through the infinite expression of Spirit that I can show you how your passed loved ones continue to love you and connect to you. We really are just two worlds working as one, getting along with dignity and respect. We have an opportunity to learn how to love one another even while physically apart. No person is separate when it comes to the link with our loved ones. Our souls are all in this together. Let this be a new soul layer revealed to you.

Sarah

Sarah passed on suddenly due to a weakened heart valve that gave out. She died young. Depression had also been a part of her life, and sometimes she would fall into a funk. She was a beautiful girl, with pale skin and silky hair. She was married, and her husband loved her very much. They had a dog together. A shared memory was of her and her sisters swimming together at a lake in Michigan. Sarah had felt chest pains for a while. When she crossed, her Uncle, who had always had coins in his pocket and would jingle his change, was waiting for her. Her grandmother was there for her too.

Her sisters, Julie, and Becky, called me for a reading. Normally, I don't read for people who have just passed, but I did in this case because her death was so sudden and such a shock to her family. They were looking for answers. I gave them all the details of her death. I told them about the heart condition that caused her death. Other evidence came pouring through...even where she had been sitting when she died. I gave this information to her sisters within twenty four hours of Sarah's death. I was told later by people who had attended the wake that my work/reading had been discussed and it had brought them great comfort. Sarah, like her sisters, was very intuitive by nature. Every time I have read for these girls in the years since, Sarah shows up with more loving information for them.

For me, it's always pretty cool to do several readings for the same family over a span of time. Energetically, I can feel how the soul coming through has changed and evolved. This shows me the higher consciousness of our souls. We continue to change and grow on the other side. I've seen how Sarah's Spirit has evolved. It's so much lighter today than it was at the first reading. This reading amazed me due to the realization that one minute she had been here on Earth, and in the blink of an eye had crossed. Then she came back within twenty four hours to tell me about it.

My 9/10 and how it prepared me for 9/11

Spirit quite often comes through to prepare me for news that I'm going to receive, or incidents that are going to occur. It can be a blessing, but it can also bring sadness when it happens. I do prefer to get a heads up from Spirit though, so I can get ready for whatever unforeseen event is about to happen. Remember, I never read myself. I'm human and have to live life just like everyone else. There are no special breaks for mediums!

Prior to September 11th, I got flashes of planes crashing. I would feel heavy, distraught, and sad. I sensed that energy was unfolding for some big event; I just didn't know what to do with it. I didn't know when the psychic press release was going to download.

I thought at the time that maybe my husband, who

traveled two weeks of the month, was going to get in a plane crash. I would find myself driving and starting to cry for no reason. I felt a deep, unexplained heartache.

The week before what has come to be called 9/11 occurred, Tom was scheduled to go to California on Flight 11. He often took an early flight across the country, coast to coast, to go to work. His plans changed the week before and he was sent to St. Louis, Missouri for a trade show instead. He left on the Sunday morning of September 10th. On that day I also had a lot planned. I was going to my Spiritual Circle group. Glen Edwards, a medium from England, was coming and we were going to train with him.

That evening, all twelve of us participating in the workshop were feeling really off in our messages. In a circle, that rarely happens. We kept getting bizarre information. Some of us were seeing President Bush with fire around him. Some were seeing firemen and stairs. We saw buildings crashing and terrified people.

No one had the nerve to ask why we were getting this information or how we were supposed to use it. To be honest, I thought we were just having an off night until the next morning when I got a call from my husband. He told me the news about the attack on the World Trade Center and to stay out of Boston. I knew then what all of our visions had meant the night before in circle. I stayed out of the city. Every city was afraid that they would be next, and people were bailing out of Boston, trying to get home.

The commute took most people hours. Energetically, I wanted to throw up. I knew what my vision had meant and what the universe was preparing me for. Just as the rest of the world did when hearing about this terrorist attack, I just cried and prayed, and cried and prayed some more.

It took Tom and four guys driving from the middle of our country twenty eight hours to get home. He drove straight through, only stopping as he dropped men off in Ohio, Pennsylvania, New York, and even one at the Canadian border. No one could get rental cars. Luckily Tom already had one, so all his co-workers piled in. Not once did they see a State Trooper or Policeman during that long ride home. They were all in their own towns, protecting their borders for fear of a terrorist attack in their own cities.

I returned to my Spiritual Class the following Sunday only to find Glenn still here. He couldn't get back to England any time soon. As our class began, we made sense of the messages we had gotten the week before. We meditated and worked at beginning to heal our country. We than began to receive Spirit. People who were victims of the tragedy were coming through. I was dumbstruck. I had never had an experience like this before. I literally couldn't move out of my chair.

That night as I drove home, I knew I was in the right career. I was asked to do this work and I honored myself by accepting. I gave thanks to God right then and there for letting me be a medium.

My son Matthew was five when 9/11 happened. Six months later he said to me, "Ya know Mom, when I was five and that plane accident happened it changed my life FOREVER." I said "You're right Matthew, it changed my life too."

Sometimes You are the Medium

I do workshops on mediumship. At the end of class, I always open up and give messages. Here's a story about what happened after one of those classes.

Barbara's Reading

During this reading, I connected with a man who had just died. His name was John. He had a terrible childhood. I found myself slamming my fists together, back and forth. This was the example he was giving me of how his stepfather used his "iron fists" as he grew up.

John was emphasizing to Barb that he appreciated their intimacy and friendship, and that his passing was due to a lifetime of issues, not just the events that had led up to his suicide. He had passed a month before this reading. He also talked about a "rocky road." He used this term a lot in his lifetime. He talked about her son Andrew, and he made reference to her grieving.

Barbara called me a few days later and thanked me for the reading. She then went on to tell me that when she got home from my class that night, there had been a message on her machine. It said "Hi Barb, I just wanted to tell you that you've been on my mind lately and also in my dreams." The caller then described the dream she had had. In the dream, she and Barb were at a wedding and they looked out into the audience. It was empty except for Pat, an old friend that had died years ago.

Here's the interesting part. The woman who had left the message had called the wrong number, and the wrong Barbara! Barbara called the woman back and gave her my number. I did a reading for the "wrong number" caller and connected her to Pat. How is that for Spirit using the communication lines? Often when we have a reading, we turn out to be a messenger too!

Our Dog Kayleigh

We keep Pembroke Welsh corgis as pets. They are the smartest, coolest dogs we've ever owned. Kayleigh was our first corgi. She lived to be twelve years old, but had become quite ill toward the end of her life. There's little worse than having a sick pet and knowing you'll have to put them down to ease their pain. Again, Spirit prepared me. A few months before, I kept having dreams of picking out puppies. I knew then that Kayleigh was going to get a grim diagnosis. She had a cancerous tumor and was suffering with diabetes.

The day we took her to the vet for her shot, I had a long talk with her. I said "Kayleigh, I love you. You have been such a good dog to our family. You have two things to do for me. You have to let me know you made it to Heaven, and you have to send the kids a puppy."

You see, I had called every breeder I knew, and every one I'd been referred to, and it appeared there wasn't a single corgi to be found. It sometimes takes as long as twelve months to get a Pembroke Welsh corgi, as they're a less common breed here in the States. Queen Elizabeth of England keeps this breed, which is why they've been nicknamed the "Queen's dog." I knew the kids would be devastated. They loved this dog very much and had never known life without her. When Haley was two, she got into the magic markers and marked up my walls everywhere she walked. Then she colored on Kayleigh, who didn't complain at all. That's how sweet this little dog had been with the kids.

As we drove to the vet, I could hear her eating McDonald's french fries from the van floor. Normally, I would have been telling her to stop, but this time I just let her find the fries and eat away. Kayleigh loved to eat fries and in that moment I didn't mind. Thinking back now, I wish I had gone to the McDonald's drive-thru and gotten her a happy meal. But at the time, I had been too distraught to think. I couldn't even talk. It's never easy to put an animal down, even when you know it's the kindest thing to do.

I was in tears and my throat was so tight I could barely breathe. As she was being put down, my husband and I patted her. In my mind I was saying "Kayleigh, go into the light. You were such a good dog here on Earth." Dr. Krump, our vet, was saying the exact same words into Kayleigh's ear and she quietly drifted off to sleep. She had such a beautiful death, surrounded by love. Now we had to go home and break the news to the kids, and with no new puppy in sight. This was not going to be an easy task.

I was right about how the kids would react. They were devastated and knew there would be no new puppies for a long time. That Friday night at 10:15, I got a call from Donna Gilbert, a breeder from Stanford, Connecticut. She told me she had just had a cancellation for a female puppy, a red and white, just like Kayleigh. "Would we want her?" she asked. "Of course!" I screamed. We could have her in three weeks. Soon Maxine would come into our lives. She would turn out to be just as sweet and gentle as Kayleigh had been.

When Monday mornings came around, Kayleigh's routine had been to announce (bark) that the school bus was here, walk the kids down to the bus, herd them onto the bus, (corgis are herding dogs) and get a few pats from the bus driver. Then she'd turn around and return home. Our first Monday morning without her was really tough. Our routine had changed and the kids felt it. That afternoon, I was waiting for Matt's bus to pick him up for school. The bus pulled into the cul-de-sac and I could hear Kayleigh barking! No other dogs were in this neighborhood, and cats don't bark! Let's face it. Your dog's bark is like your baby's cry. You'd know it anywhere. Right away I said "Thank you for my sign Kayleigh."

My daughter Avery, who was four at the time, took her death the hardest. I should have known how sensitive this child was going to be. One night that same year, I was giving her a bath when she asked "Mom, do you know I have visions." I said "You do?" and then asked "What kind of vision do you have?" She replied "About the future. Do you have visions Mom?" I told her that yes, I did. "It's good to have visions Ave. Does it scare you?" I asked. "No, it doesn't." she answered. What an enlightened conversation to be having with such a little girl!

As Matthew's bus pulled up, Avery said "Mom! I hear Kayleigh dog barking!" I said "Me too Ave. See, Kayleigh's in Heaven right now letting us know she's okay." That was the last time we ever heard her bark. As we were walking up the street to the house Avery asked "What is Kayleigh going to have for dinner tonight Mom?" I replied "McDonald's french fries." She just laughed and laughed and said "Silly Kayleigh Dog. She loved french fries."

Animals, just like people, do come back to give us messages. They are unconditionally connected to our love and want to let us know that they're O.K. Another layer unveiled. I've done plenty of readings where dogs, cats, and even horses, have come back to link with their owners. They don't come through and say "Hey Frank! How ya doing?" but they do give evidence of their lives, and of you and your relationship with them. It can be about the color of their fur, the place you walked them, the place they slept, or another animal they were friendly with; evidence that only you as their owner would know. Animals have the most magical energy. They love us all the time, and even in death they still manage to comfort us. We are so blessed by them, aren't we? They're just the purest of love, so of course they want to let us know that they're doing fine in their new home. They also want us to know that we'll be O.K. (well, kind of O.K.) without them.

Uncle Michael

Spirits have a way of making themselves known. One night while I was sleeping, I saw a man by my bed pacing back and forth. Yes, I know, this happens to everyone, doesn't it? He was a short, stocky, Irish looking fellow. I knew it was Uncle Michael.

This man wasn't a relative of mine, but of my good friend Rosie. If he could have shook the bed he would have! There was an urgent energy to his demeanor. No surprise there, as it was two am and he still wanted me to "hop to it" and get right to work as a medium.

Like I said before, I don't think they have the same clocks in Heaven. They must be in reverse of ours because their timing is so off! I woke up the next morning and called Rosie. She greeted me with a happy "Good morning!" I said "Uncle Michael was in my room last night." She laughed and asked "What did he want?"

Uncle Michael had not been happy with his will and the family antics that ensued after he passed. It's really unfortunate how often greed takes over in some families. Rosie and Uncle Michael were close. They truly loved one another. Uncle Michael had no children, so Rosie's children were like his grandchildren. The other thing about Uncle Michael was that he had been a very intuitive man. He and Rosie could connect this way very easily. It came as no surprise that Uncle Michael would be throwing evidence at me about his passing, the timing of his passing, the cover up involving his will, and even about a spoon that dropped off a table. I knew that some of it was obscure evidence. The spoon drop happened when Rosie attended his wake and was sitting at a table with all of the family that would eventually be fighting over his land and money. Uncle Michael was pretty specific in his details.

I often wondered, as the details came out over the next two years, if Uncle Michael had wanted to hit a few of them with that spoon. Boy, was he ever pissed about how they handled things. I wish I had a better ending to this story, but as it turned out, the wrong people benefited from his will. The greed was particularly bad in this case. The only condolence that Rosie has is that Uncle Michael will be discussing "the situation" with a few of them at the Pearly Gates.

The message in Uncle Michael's story is to always remember that you reap what you sow, even in Spirit. It's like I always say to my kids "Play nice." Sometimes adults need to remember that too, but many don't and act rude and inconsiderate instead.

An interesting side note to this story; when I called Rosie to ask if I could include Uncle Michael's story in my book I said "Rosie, Uncle Michael was on my mind and all around me again today. She said "Me too. You know why?" "No," I answered. She then told me that the day I called her was the anniversary of Uncle Michael's passing. I thought it was pretty cool that I wrote this story on his anniversary, and then thought

"Look at that persistent Irishman! At least he didn't wake me up in the wee hours of the night this time!" Don't you just love how Spirit works?

Jane

Jane was the woman I mentioned earlier, who had the heartache of knowing she was getting ready to pass with breast and lung cancer. It had been spreading quickly when she came to me for a second reading. I knew when I saw her, that this would be the last time. It broke my heart to know that I was reading for this woman as she was in her final stages of cancer. When she walked into my office, she had her young daughter with her who was all of 10 years old.

I was shocked to think that I would be reading her with her daughter there, but that was all part of Jane's plan. She had not told me she was bringing her! The real point of her visit was to help her daughter understand that her life would continue, and that they would still be connected and together. She would just be watching over her as an angel.

I could not have had enough tissues in that room. Not for them, but FOR ME! I was being bombarded by her loved ones coming through and comforting her, plus I was feeling both her and her daughter's pain and anguish. My energy was a mess. It was by far the hardest reading I have ever done. Symbolically, I kept getting tulip flowers and springtime. Jane then told me she had planted those flowers, as she wanted something of her to come back to life every year for her daughter. This reading went on for almost two hours, with talking, crying, and laughing. The whole time this young girl was so strong and accepting. I was amazed at the dignity that Jane had instilled into the process of death for her daughter. She showed her by example not to fear it, that it was just another part of life. She modeled for her daughter acceptance and the trust in love that we all need during the most difficult moments in our lives.

During this appointment, we talked about what Heaven would be like for Mom, and how to pay attention to the signs that they would share once she had crossed. We discussed how there will always be love, and also life; just like those tulips of hers that would come up year after year. In death our souls teach us many lessons. This young child will have those memories of her mother being independent and strong, and showing her that in life you can handle anything; even death itself.

Peace, Love, and Light to you, beautiful Jane, and thank you for that day. As hard as it was for me to read through all my tears, you showed me the beautiful gift of true grace.

XO Kelle

Everything Disney

Spirit often gives me images when I'm doing a reading. Sometimes these images are a bit bizarre, but I just go with it because I've learned to trust their guidance. I know they are always right.

One day, a little old man with a beard walked up my stairs and I wondered "What will *this* reading bring?" It turned out Fred would become my oldest client at eighty-five years old; another affirmation that whether young and old, people want to connect to their loved ones. This work is not just a young person game. Everyone is a player, according to Spirit.

I began my reading with Fred, and his beloved wife came through with evidence that only he would know: His passion for chocolate and candy; an ashtray that fell off a shelf; her complaints about his pipe smoking, and wanting to make sure he smoked outside, not inside, the house. She confirmed that she was visiting him and yes, that those visits were real. All this great evidence of her was coming through in the reading, but as the reading progressed, I suddenly kept seeing Walt Disney's face. I was seeing remembered images of taking my kids to Disney World when they were little. It was the weirdest thing, and a bit distracting! At the same time, I was also seeing paintbrushes, canvas paintings, and drawings, so I knew this man worked in art.

But, like I've said, Spirit always knows best. Come to find out Fred...is...Pluto! He worked for Walt himself, and helped design the favorite dog of all time, known to us as Mickey's dog Pluto!

One of the messages Fred's beautiful wife gave him was that she wanted him to get back to painting. When we're grieving, it can be so hard to get back to our hobbies, or the other things we enjoy. I could sense he really wanted to retire his paintbrushes, but his wife was strongly encouraging him to continue to live and enjoy his life.

It's been a few years since I connected for Fred. He was a delight to read for. The other day in the mail I got a brochure advertising his paintings. He has now returned to living and following his passion. Wouldn't his wife and Walt Disney be proud? Go Fred!

Spirit is there for all of us, no matter our age or circumstance. They're always looking out for us. Our link to them is the same as it was here on Earth. There is a great vibration in this life. It's called love. It's the feeling of pureness, and it's the emissary that shows us how to live our lives. That guidance will always, always, link us back to our loved ones who have passed on. This soul layer is what enables us to stay connected, even after death. Our loved ones are our ambassadors to the other side, loving us and sending us their messages. Sometimes they come in our dreams, sometimes through coincidences, and sometimes through messages from a medium. Whatever method, they'll get to us. They'll always find a way.

Please keep your senses and heart open. Your loved ones may, at any given moment, have the opportunity to reveal themselves to you, so listen.

Remember the game we all played as kids, *I Spy?* Have you ever played *I Spy* with Spirit? Well, I have and I recommend it!

My friend Cheryl had recently lost her mother after a long, long illness and transition.

Soon after, she called me while cleaning out her mother's home. Many of us have been through the difficult process of finding the treasures and the "not really" treasures left behind. It's one tough job, as you know if you've ever been through it.

As I was on the phone with her, just gabbing away, both her mom and dad come through. Now mind you, Cheryl and I are very connected. We may not see each other often, but when we do it's always as if we just talked the day before. Both of our fathers were diagnosed with Stage 4 Cancer within weeks of each other, and they also died within 24 hours of one another. How's that for coincidence? We went through a lot in those five months. We were able to lean on each other in our time of grief.

It would be quite appropriate for her mom and dad to "butt in" on our conversation. When her mom came through, she started showing me evidence of keys; a bunch of them together on a ring. I saw them in the kitchen. Turns out, Cheryl was sitting in the kitchen and the keys were right in front of her. Mom started giving me information about her death, and how important it was for her daughter to understand that it was okay that she wasn't there when she died. Cheryl was in Florida at the time, taking her kids on the traditional Disney World vacation. She had gone on vacation with her mother's blessing, but had still been feeling uneasy about going. Remember what I have said before, that whoever is supposed to be there will be there. No one needs to get hung up on the last moment of the process.

Her mother wanted to ease Cheryl's conscious and let her know that it was okay to let all of that go. It wasn't important and she had no need for regrets. I know this comforted Cheryl. There were lots of other details Mom gave to her that also aided with her grief. Next, Dad came through to tell her how much he loves her. He also kept telling me to tell her to look under the bed! Huh, what? Okay... so I told Cheryl that he wants her to look under the bed.

Cheryl's parents were savers. And by that I mean they saved everything! I think that's common with the depression generation because my folks were the same way. I remember when I cleaned out my mom's house and found a Fry Daddy that was purchased in 1970. It was the same scene for Cheryl, but her parents' clutter went to the extreme. She even found multiple sets of false teeth! We would laugh and she would say "Who keeps other people's false teeth?" During the hunt for things in the house, they looked for jewelry, toys, yearbooks, pictures, and... false teeth. (Ha! Ha! Just kidding!)

Her dad started screaming in my ear, again pushing me to tell Cheryl to look under the bed. "Okay!" I said to him, "I'll tell her!" So I said to her "Go look under your dad's bed," and she admitted to me that she's afraid of what she might find. She walked into her dad's bedroom anyway, and looked under the bed. She yelled "The typewriter! We've been looking for that!" "I spy a typewriter," her dad then whispered in my ear.

Check the Glovey

As a psychic I often get asked to find things. My daughter Avery is great at this. She's the finder in my house so whenever something goes missing, we ask Ave because she'll know where it is. Remember, we all have those hunches and gut instincts, an inner voice that answers our questions. We've all asked ourselves "Where are my darn car keys?" and heard a voice telling us right where to look. I found mine in the fridge once, I kid you not. Sometimes I get asked to help locate lost jewelry or items of sentimental value. A friend of mine, told me that his wife had lost her ring. She had searched everywhere for it. A few of my psychic friends gave our best to help her find it. I tuned into this ring and asked where it was. I kept seeing a car and then I heard "Check the glovey." (Glove compartment) Sure enough, when the car was checked and the glove compartment opened, the ring was there! Whether it's a missing person case, giving a message, or finding someone's ring, I'm constantly being given evidence through my intuition and by working with Spirit.

Everything Has Meaning

You know by now that I'm ALL about following signs and symbols. I talk a lot about this on my radio show every week. I explain how to keep your psychic ability in check and real in your life because, guess what? IT IS. Everything has a meaning for us. As a psychic medium, I can't emphasize this enough. Pay attention on a daily, and sometimes even an hourly, basis. We are all creatures of habit. How many of us read our daily horoscope, but don't bother to look for messages during our day, or better yet, act on them?

Right now I'm telling you to blow off your horoscope. Instead, open up your mind through meditation, and then look for signs and guidance concerning situations you face during your day. Have you ever opened a book to a random page and found information that was strangely helpful or that even gave you an "Aha!" moment? All you techies out there with your computer tablets full of this and that might miss out on this little adventure, but I'm sure Spirit will find a way to work with you and your computers all the same! Just ask your guides for a sign today and see what happens. Remember, we're all energy, and the energy from Spirit will always find us. Pay attention to TV ads, songs on the radio, etc. Signs can come to us through all forms of communication. I'm just a really big "toucher" and like the feel of a book and its paper. I know this is becoming a lost art, but I still prefer paper and pen. In fact, this book was all hand written before it was typed. That's how old school I am! My energy can be too high when it comes to electronics. I can't help it. I've actually been known to burn up electronic devices! When I moved into my current home, we had seven power outages in ten days. No joke. It took a little while for the North Shore to get used to me, but it's all good now. These days it only happens when there's a real storm!

I try to motor down when I get on a computer. I also never get the remote in my house, so I can't turn the channel. The "clicker" won't work for me. My kids know to change the station for me. It's all just part of my lovely vibration. Oh well. As far as mediums go, this is pretty common.

One wintery Saturday, I had to drop my kids off early in the morning for some activities they were participating in. On the way, I noticed a sign for an estate sale a few blocks from my house. Estate sales, bakeries, and butchers are always on my radar. I can be anywhere and sniff them out! I dropped into the estate sale on my way back. Most things were pretty picked over, (I hate that!) but the collection of books were phenomenal. I could tell that the person who lived there was someone I could have had days and days of conversation with. In fact, I soon did! The man was still hanging around the house in Spirit and was telling me that he was not at all happy with how his family was handling the sale. It was a "grab and go" type of sale; the daughter would just shout out a price and then people would give her the money. His Spirit was not pleased, and his energy kept following me around. He was very frustrated. The way the sale was being conducted really was in poor taste, and showed total disrespect for this man's prize possessions. It was as if it was all just being pawned out. It made us both sad. He did tell me how happy he was about the books I was choosing though, and glad they were going into a happy home with someone that would appreciate them. (Yes, I had a conversation with a ghost while at an estate sale!) I found books from the 1930's on mysticism, celebrating the solstice, and the power of the feminine. I was like a psychic kid in a candy store! I got four books for three dollars! Bargain of the day, and the knowledge? Priceless.

One of the books I picked up was an 1100 page book called *The Woman's Encyclopedia* of *Myths and Secrets* by *Barbara G. Walker*. It's one of those books that can just mesmerize you with all the weird and true facts. This book actually inspired me to write about *Alchemy and the Teenager,* which will be my next book. See how signs, symbols, and coincidences work together? Everything in life always has a reason, whether good or bad. It's important to play with Spirit, and take the inspiration they can give to us. Be open to them and they'll give you those signs all the time.

One afternoon, I picked up that estate sale book, *The Women's Encyclopedia of Myths and Secrets,* and said "Give me some inspiration." I opened that huge book, pulled back the pages, and pointed. I looked twice and couldn't believe what I saw! To my great surprise, there was my name, spelled K-E-L-L-E, on page 498 of an 1100 page encyclopedia!

I have to tell you how significant this is to me. I've been dealing with the unusual spelling of my name forever. Everyone wants to spell it with a Y at the end because that's how it's pronounced. My parents wanted it to be spelled differently. It was *so* different it turns out, that as a kid I was never able to have the pencils or bike plates with my name on them. When you're seven that's a big deal! Once when I was young, my dad went to a political fundraiser. The man who was running for representative had the last name of *Kelley*. My dad took the bumper sticker and cut off the Y. I kept that sticker on my bedroom door for as long as I can remember. I think it was still there when I got married! My dad was always one to make do with things, which was lucky for me. As a kid, I was just thrilled to have something printed with my name on, just like every other Mary, Susan or Karen.

I'm a firm believer that as children, we pick our parents, pick our identities, and even pick our names, which become a part of us. So to all of you adults out there who want to complain about your parents giving you a horrible name, they didn't. You picked your name and even the way it's spelled. It was preordained from your soul. I believe I was meant to have my name. Keeping in mind that before now I have never, in my forty eight years, *ever* seen the meaning of my name, here is its meaning as I found it in my book:

1. Kelle - Irish (I'm Irish) druid priest. Name derived from pre-Christian, holy harlots (Hmmm...) of the Goddess Kelle, Kale or Kali. Irish writings described the divine harlot Mary Magdalene as a Kelle. The medieval term Kele-Dewas, considered mysterious, translates to "bride of God" if a woman, or "servant of God" if a man.

2. These translations were inaccurate. Kele-De meant literally the spirit of the Goddess Kele, evidently identical with the Goddess Kali of the original Indo - European Celts. Votaries of the Goddess Kele stressed the search inward, and perfection through meditation, yogic style.

3. Her Gods assumed the lotus position like eastern yogis. (The "Psychic Cup of Calm" that I preach) Her primitive Grail, her Peredur, experienced her as the most

beautiful woman in the world (Why thank you!) represented by the three colors of the Divine Prakriti, still known as Gunas, standing for her powers of creation, preservation, and destruction.

4. The Mythical "St. Kilda" seems to have another version of the Goddess Kele, dwelling on a remote rocky inlet once identified with the western paradise of the DEAD. (I kid you not.) St. Kilda's Isle still exists, but the origin of its name has been forgotten. The ubiquitous Irish word kill, or cell, or cave, once meant a shrine of Kele, whose holy men called themselves "Culdees." Some were described in Christian histories as monks, though they were obviously married.

5. Kildare was a major shrine of the Goddess Kilda-Kele, or Brigit, identified with the Virgin Mary after Christian monks appropriated the site.

(Guess how many rocks I sat on in County Kildare in Ireland while visiting? I was just grabbing the energy from the land, not knowing that it was the land of my namesake.)

This is a good example of how Spirit gives us signs and symbols meant to influence us. I was so thrilled to find this definition of my name. I called my mom, who is eighty-five, and reminded her why she named me what she did! She said "Well Kelle, that sure sounds like you, except for the harlot part!" I had to agree with her.

I invite you to look up your name and see what you find and why you picked it; it may have more meaning than you think!

A Touch of Evil

Yep, I'm saying the word. I hate that word, but I'm using it in this story so you can understand what it means. I touched a piece of evil. I'm not proud of it, but this is one crazy story that even surprised me.

There's a practice that psychics use called psychometry. This is when a psychic holds an object and picks up energy from it. For some psychics and mediums, it helps ground the energy they're working with.

It can be an object a person wore, like jewelry, or a picture of the person you are reading. I personally don't usually need an object to hold in order to read because I can often pick up information from objects without holding them. Once in a while though I will use objects, especially when I'm doing a missing persons case. This can assist in the process of gathering information.

Everything is made of energy and leaves a psychic imprint. This is how objects hold the vibrations of the "who, what, where, when, or how" of the information itself.

When psychics are tested for their abilities by universities, the test objects will often be placed in envelopes and hidden so that the psychic can't see them. The psychic's job is to then do a psychic press release and give details of what's in the envelope. They do this in order to test the mind's eye and to see if the psychic can actually reveal any information.

Here's my experience with touching evil. A friend of mine, Linda, called me and asked me if I can read objects by holding them. I said "I usually don't but, yeah, I can read objects that way." She then invited me over. As soon as I walked into her kitchen she handed me a faceted, clear, crystal the size of a nickel. I asked what it was and she said "You tell me."

As soon as I picked it up, my guides whispered "Don't pick it up. Throw it down." I said to Linda, "I'm not supposed to pick this up." But I did it anyway. I know that our curiosity can get us into trouble sometimes. I wish I had listened to my intuition.

I held the crystal. It had come from an old mine and was very old itself. It had a unique and ancient history. I saw military. I remember saying "Is this related to that Osama Bin Laden crap?" It definitely had an evil presence and carried really, really bad energy. I was seeing a huge estate that was very broken down. I felt that the crystal came from someplace far away from where I was standing. Finally, when I started to see images of mass murder, I stopped and said "What the hell is this?"

She told me I was holding a crystal from a chandelier that had been in Saddam Hussein's palace. Here I was in Andover, Massachusetts, touching a piece of evil from another country. Right away I wanted to cleanse my whole body with sage and lavender, and pray. After a few glasses of wine with my friend to ease the stress I had felt from that evil dictator's chandelier, I did just that.

How did she get this crystal, and how did I end up holding something from such a horrific dictator? Linda's brother, who was in the army, had been in Iraq. He was there when the palace of Saddam Hussein was taken. As most soldiers do, he looked for relics to bring home from the war. There were crystals on the floor from a chandelier when his platoon overtook the palace, so he scooped them up and brought them back to America.

What did Linda do with the crystal? She threw it in the trash! This was a wise move, as no one needs that kind of evil energy in their home. No thank you!

One of my favorite sayings is by the spiritual teacher, Hildegard of Bingen:

"We cannot live in a world

that is interpreted for us by others.

An interpreted world is not a hope.

Part of the terror is to take back our own listening.

To use our own voice.

To see our own light".

Hildegard Bingen is a Saint in the Catholic Church. She wrote theological, botanical, and medical texts, as well brilliant poems. She was born in 1098 and was a woman way before her time. Her inspirations are as relevant today as they were back in the 11th century.

Saddam Hussein should have been inspired by Hildegard Bingen. Maybe things could have been different. Maybe his mind wouldn't have been so evil, and thousands of people would not have been killed under his regime. We all know that his soul must be in a very dark place on the other side. It resides in one of the lowest planes of soul living, and that's not a place any of us would want to enter. I think Hitler is probably his roommate.

Boston Marathon - April 15, 2013

This is one very sad day to have experienced and to remember. It's still so raw for the Boston community and for our country. I was at the airport at 5 am that day, taking my family on a spring break vacation. We were off to our first island trip to Antigua. I kept hearing the guides in my head screaming at me "911! 911! 911!" I knew then that something was going to happen at the marathon that day. I had also predicted years ago that the Marathon would be hit by terrorism. When you get these premonitions, it's a feeling of being a "sitting duck" and not knowing which way to turn with the information. I just prayed for the city and asked for protection for me and my family as we traveled. When we got on the plane, Haley and Avery said to me "Mom, did you put the Christ light around the plane?" Christ light is a spiritual light and the God presence of protection. For safety, I always envision it around a plane when I travel. I told the girls that of course I had. Haley looked back at me and nervously said "Mom, really, did you do it? Do it again." I could tell she was feeling something, and that her psychic antenna was up.

We landed in beautiful Antigua around two o'clock. We went off to find the Nonsuch Bay Resort, where we would be staying. When we checked in I discovered our villa's room number was 911. I am not joking. I knew then that I had gotten my confirmation that something was happening. My husband Tom got on the internet an hour or so later and said "Kelle, there's been a bombing at the marathon!" My heart sank. My daughter Haley said "Mom, the reason I kept having you put the Christ light around the plane was because I kept seeing bombs go off!"

Holy crap. Haley had told Avery about her thoughts. That's why they had been so nervous that morning. Not only had there been one psychic antenna going up at Logan Airport that day, there had been three!

Had we not left for vacation, Avery would have been at the marathon that day with some of her track mates, cheering everyone on at the finish line. That group of kids had left the race an hour before it happened. Unfortunately, some of the kids from Andover had stayed and been injured. Although we were in this beautiful part of the world, we felt uneasy and sad the whole time. I kept sending healing and prayers back to our city of Boston while sitting on the beach. Like the rest of the world, all I could do was keep praying. When people found out where we were from, they were so sorry and empathetic. We were gifted with such a sense of community and love that I wanted to cry every time someone expressed kind words to me.

The whole world felt the effects of the Boston Marathon tragedy, but some more than others. When I got back home a week after it happened, I did my radio show on as usual. I talked all about premonitions, and what had happened energetically to the Boston community.

I knew at the time that at least two or three more people would be caught in connection to this bombing.

The next day they announced just that.

CHAPTER 12   ALL IN A GHOST HUNT

In the summer of 2009, my good friend Linda asked me to go on a ghost hunt with her. I have to admit I really didn't want to go, for the good Lord knows, I see enough of them already. I certainly don't need to go hunting for more!

It's true that I can feel spirits wherever I go. It can be in a hair salon, a pub, someone's home, or a castle in London. I don't dwell on it, and it doesn't frighten me. It's just a fact of my life. I simply acknowledge them and then send them on their way.

When Linda, who's not a medium but does have strong intuition, invited me to go with her I thought "Okay, but what am I getting myself into? I wonder if I'll be scared." How funny! The medium who talks to dead people wondering if she'll be afraid of the dead! Hey, I'm normal. Just like anyone else, I don't like getting spooked! I had no idea what to expect from the evening, but off we went to the Haverhill Historical Buttonwoods Museum. It was equipped with old everything, and conveniently located right next door to a cemetery. Just great!

I had no idea that a ghost hunt would have such a huge following. Hundreds of people showed up with EVP recordings and headlamps. I had nothing to use to light my way, but good ole' Linda had her brought her cell phone, so we were good! We had no idea what we were getting into.

Our ghost hunter directors for the evening were two English mediums: Gavin Cromwell and David Wells of the television show *Most Haunted.* I thought "Well, I guess we're in good hands." Remember, I'd never been down this road before, but there are always firsts in my line of work, and never a dull moment!

It was a whole evening made up of people getting into groups, being guided into parts of the museum and cemetery, and giving their impressions of what they felt, sensed, and observed. Included on the property was an old house named "The 1710 John Ward House." It had been transplanted onto the property. There was "gobs" of spirit activity. Oh, and did I mention that Girl and Boy Scout groups had sleepovers in that old house? Are you kidding me? Talk about spiritually active! There's no way that *I* would have wanted to stay the night in there, never mind a bunch of little kids! I'm sure they'll need nightlights in their bedrooms for the rest of their lives! When I was in that house, so many spirits showed up that even I was surprised. Then one medium on our tour decided to channel and talk in tongues. They scared the living crap out of my friend! She grabbed on to me and held my hand so tight I thought she would break it! I kept thinking "What am I doing in this place?!" Can you imagine seven to ten year old kids in this environment? Whose idea was *that*?

Whenever there's a lot of old stuff in an area, there will be residual energy hanging out. That's why all you antique collectors out there should clear the objects that you're bringing into your homes. It's the same concept as when you buy a new house, and then clear it and bless it to make it yours.

I was in a museum full of old, old stuff that had not been cleared. Some of it dated back to the original American Indians and the birth of America. My energy was bouncing off the walls. I kept thinking "Holy cow, why did I do this?"

As I was participating, I would tell myself to just be quiet and go with the flow. I kind of wanted to be out of sight and out of mind, but Spirit had a different plan. That just wasn't in the cards for me. Spirit wanted my attention in every room I walked through. I was ready to blow a psychic gasket. And it didn't take very long before that's just what I did!

These wonderful gentlemen were giving the tour and people were trying to find proof of a ghost or haunting. I started piping up and adding my psychic two cents worth to the event. I couldn't help myself, and I really didn't feel like I had a choice. Before I knew it, it had become the "Gavin, David and Kelle Tour." They were pointing out evidence, and I was pointing out evidence, as well as communicating from Spirit.

There was a young Indian girl hiding in one of the rooms we went into. I saw her running, and she told me her heart was pounding and that she couldn't get away. She was very young, maybe five or six years old, and she wanted to get back to her family; especially to her mother. I knew she had been killed, as my head was starting to throb and I was feeling it in a very physical way. I had tears stinging my eyes because I could feel her loss and frightened emotions.

The curator of the museum confirmed for me that Native American children used to be chased and stoned to death here, sometimes as sport. I can't even fathom that kind of brutality. I sent the little girl into the light, healing that little angel as she went off to the other side, to finally be with her mother again. It was amazing. The whole time I was ghost hunting, all four hours, I was sending first this one, then that one, into the light. I was really a very bad ghost hunter. I knew I hadn't gone there to hunt. I had gone there to cross souls over the veil so they could move on. I didn't want them to stay in that old museum. I wanted them to go where they were supposed to be, in Heaven. I wanted them to go into that beautiful dimension. I wanted them to be healed. While everyone else was looking for evidence and EVPing it up, I had already confirmed that yes indeed, there were ghosts there. I had gotten all the evidence I needed. Now it was time for their energy to crossover so I told them to boogie on outta there!

One of the strangest things that happened involved a haunted mirror that I saw when I walked into one of the other rooms there. First, the room got really cold. Normally my body temperature is on fire. My red Irish cheeks are always showing their true color when I work. The breeze actually felt good to me. There was a woman there with me who had a camera on her. I told her what I was feeling, and that I saw a spirit cowering in the corner. This spirit was being confined there.

She snapped a picture of the room and in the mirror was a face. I saw the picture, and the woman said she thought it had demonic overtones. I thought "GREAT. What am I doing here again?" I hate any kind of devil stuff, and true to my Catholic upbringing, I started to pray to Mary. Trust me, a "Hail Mary" or two can come in handy at a moment like this! Then my mother instinct kicked in and I couldn't just leave that poor spirit behind. I put my "big medium panties" on, and sent healing to the room and to the spirit cowering in the corner. I told them it was safe to leave. There's something that people need to understand; negative spirit can hold a positive spirit in place. There's a kind of entrapment that can happen, especially with very old energy. Keep in mind that two or three hundred years ago, life was very puritanical. Your religious beliefs were everything. If you ever did anything out of the norm, you were going to go to hell, end of subject. It was very black and white thinking. You had either lived virtuously, or you hadn't. There was simply no middle ground. I truly believe that's why we have spirits choosing to hang around and not cross over. They're afraid of having to answer for their "sins." Energy gets stuck in fear and stays. I always feel it's a disservice to their souls for them to stay. God has a place for everyone. If a soul lingers, it's usually due to some fear or trauma pertaining to the way in which they died. I believe that eventually all ghosts will go where they belong. Sometimes, they just need a little push. That's where I can help, by giving them a nudge, and you can too. Don't let souls linger around you. I feel those souls have had there their time here on Earth and have used up their space. They need to be told it's not theirs anymore and that it's time to move on.

It's amazing the amount of energy that people who attend these ghost hunts expend looking for proof of spirits. I'll make it easier for you and tell you the answer. Ghosts are real. They're all around, and some stay longer than others. If you feel or sense that something's "off" about a place that you're staying, and your instincts are telling you that it may be haunted, than you're probably right. You may be sharing a room with someone you didn't plan too! Don't be scared. Send them a blessing, tell them they can't stay with you, and remind them they have somewhere else to be.

I'm a big proponent of the notion that the deceased have had their time here on Earth, and now they need to let us have ours. It's really that simple. If you don't live in this space anymore, then head on out. I even tell my kids this. They feel Spirit energy too when we're in a new place. The Sutliff family vacations usually have an interesting twist, to say the least. You must remember that you're always in control. If you feel anything out of the norm, say a prayer and send the spirits on their way. Everyone needs to understand this. Also, people need to stop welcoming ghosts into their lives just because they saw it on T.V. and think it's cool. They may inadvertently open a door that's not healthy for them. Remember, you only want good energy around you, not the bad stuff, right? We have enough living to do in our own lives. We don't need someone else's past life mucking up our own. Another soul layer revealed.

I haven't done a formal ghost hunt since that first one. I'm really not good at it. I don't need any additional evidence to prove the existence of Spirit. I've already had plenty! I want to send them all on their way because the place they're going to is where their healing will begin. (Even if they are two hundred years late!) There's always hope and goodwill awaiting every soul on their journey. It's just a matter of priorities, I guess. There are some great mediums that get their evidence while ghost hunting. They're entertained by it and like proving that ghosts do exist. There can also be big money in this field. Oh well. I'd rather be a ghost helper than a ghost hunter anyway.

Can psychic ability happen at any time in your life?

My answer to this is "Of course!" At any time in your life the psychic door can open for you. For me, it started at a young age. As I got older, I shut it off and then... Bam! I cracked that door back open and accepted that this would be part of my world. I became a professional psychic medium. That doesn't necessarily mean that you'll end up doing what I do, but it does mean that psychic gifts have been given to you. Don't be afraid to develop them and use them in your life. You and your soul have chosen psychic ability and to work with its energy. When you're ready, it will present itself.

What do I do with a child who shows

psychic promise?

The most important thing is to believe them, and to understand that what they're seeing and feeling is real. If you criticize a child and tell them that what they're feeling is wrong, over time their psychic ability will dissolve. Handle their questions with kid gloves, literally. Nurture them. Kids are great, full of promise and imagination. They know no boundaries when it comes to how they see the possibilities in life. If only adults could be more childlike; what an easy, carefree, world we would have. Sure, our bedrooms would be a mess and our "To Do" lists wouldn't get handled, but who cares? We would be happy!

How do you develop your psychic ability?

Listen, we can all tune in to some degree, but it will definitely come more easily for some than for others. It's kind of like math. Some people will have a natural talent for it, but everyone can learn it and use it. For many people, math will only be used now and then. For others, it will be the very foundation of their lives. They'll become scientists, accountants, and financial planners. Psychic ability is the same way. The best part about learning to use psychic ability is that you won't have to go to the blackboard and divide fractions in front of twenty-four people in order to do it! You won't be put on the spot with Spirit, like I was in the fourth grade with math! Thank goodness for my friend Karen Farrar who gave me the answers. (There are some things about elementary school that you just never forget!) Spirit is much nicer, and never, ever goes for the jugular when you get the answer wrong. I know, I know, I have left over Catholic School Trauma. (CST) I should really start a support group... Anyway, if you learn that you have a psychic gift, you will be one hundred percent supported. I promise you that. This is another layer revealed to you. Your guides and loved ones will be your biggest cheerleaders and will never discourage you. They want to work with you. So let's get started.

First things first, tell yourself you are willing to try. Give it your all and thank God for your gift. Please don't "hem and haw." I don't want to hear "I don't know how," or my favorite, "Is this a bad thing?" No, it's a great thing to trust your intuition and guidance. It's very healthy and whole for you to do so. Once you've accepted your new found friend known as psychic ability, the next thing you need to do is to find a teacher to work with. Look in new age spiritual stores, on the bulletin board at the health food store, at a Spiritualist church, or anyplace else you think a psychic or two might be hiding. Have conversations with them to see who is giving a class in Psychic Development. Remember, just as you would when picking out anything important to you, make sure you do your research and find something that feels right. You have to put a little skin in the game to make the world open up for you. Knowing and embracing this is also another layer revealed. You need to own your psychic gift. There are many gifted teachers out there that can help you do that. If you can't find a teacher or program in your area, go online. I offer online development classes. The internet is the greatest tool for finding education around today. But you have to be willing to take advantage of it. I wish I had had "the net" back in the day to help me! Explore it, and search out your options.

Now that you've accepted your gift and researched your tools, the last thing you'll need is practice. You know the old saying that "practice makes perfect"? Well, in my world this is one of the things that hold true. You need to give readings. Doing this will build your confidence and intuition. You did it as a kid when you played the games *I Spy*, *Charades*, and *Clue*; which was my own personal favorite, by the way. Professor Plum with the candle stick in the library was my prelude to becoming a psychic investigator. When I was ten I loved that game! I was great at all the guessing games where intuition was needed. Surprise! These are the kinds of tools I use with my kids when I host what we call "Psychic Tuesdays" at my house. I make them guess my thoughts and the objects I'm thinking about. In this way they learn to stretch their intuitive minds.

If you practice on your friends and family, you'll be amazed at how your intuition comes alive, and how accurate you'll become. You'll learn how to intuitively feel what is right and what is wrong. It's also important to try and find a circle to sit in. A circle is often found through metaphysical people. Most psychics and healers can all help you find one, as they are often participants.

Circles are the greatest tool for learning about your energy and how it works. You'll find them very powerful for getting your psychic energy to ramp up, supported by the gentle breeze of confirmation. The circle is a positive, love based group. It can aid you in becoming more in tune with your natural gift. Once you acknowledge your talents and study psychic intuition, you'll be well on your way to trusting your new best friend: You, the psychic.

Remember That Your Home is Sacred

Have you ever walked into your house (or someone else's) and the air felt heavy? If you've ever been house shopping, you'll remember that some homes felt great and welcoming, while others just felt "off" and you'd never want to live in them. The bottom line is, we feel energy in our homes and the homes we visit, whether we're conscious of it or not.

If you have an argument, don't let the tension in your home linger. That energy needs to be cleared out because if it's not, it will fester and bleed into your own energy. It becomes "dirty" energy. It's kind of like not showering for a week. I don't know who would do that, but you can imagine how great you'd feel when you finally got clean. Yikes! You get the picture, right? Well think of years and years of unclean energy hanging out in your home. It can get pretty stale.

In the most dramatic cases of bad energy, a murder or some other kind of violence took place in the house. If a home like this is never cleared or prayed over, it will be tainted with negativity for a long, long time. I can remember that when I was growing up, people would often have a priest or minister come to bless a house. It was an automatic ritual. We bless our babies when they're born. Why don't we bless the new beginnings in our homes? I want everyone to get back into this practice and bless their dwellings. The place you live is your most sacred space. You eat, sleep, bathe, love, and breathe in your home. If the energy is off, you will be too. Your mental and physical balance is the key to a good life, and the structure in which you live should be honored; another soul layer revealed.

Here's my recipe for clearing the energy in your home so all the "dirty energy" gets out and stays out! I have done this for years and I can tell you that most people feel very comfortable in my home. You have to work at keeping your home's energy healthy. Native Americans believed in the powerful energy of cleansing their land. I also strongly believe in this practice. They would use lavender and white sage. You should always try to grow these two plants on your property. Now that you've secured the outside, it's time to work on the inside.

When you clear your home, you will need a few things:

1. A lavender candle.

2. White sage stick.

3. Your prayers.

First, light your candle and place it in the center of your home. Often this will be your kitchen. Isn't that where all the action usually is? Next, say a prayer to God, the Universe, or any holy name you personally refer to. I always call in God and Archangels (the big guns: Michael, Uriel, Raphael, and Gabriel) to assist in clearing. I state my intentions and ask that all negative energy leave my home, and that my home stay in balance "for the highest and best good of my healthy home." Amen.

Lastly, burn the sage stick. A word of warning - it smells like pot. The first time I ever cleared my home I remember hearing "What's that smell?" Sniff, sniff... The lavender candle will diminish the smell so it won't last long. Walk from room to room with the sage stick burning. When you finish with this clearing, blow out the sage stick and let the lavender candle remain burning. Your home will feel lighter, warm and inviting; just how a home should feel. All those years of stress buildup, washed away! It's really this easy. Your home is free and clear of negative energy.

HALLELUJAH!

Sweet Dreams Everyone, and Sweet Remembrance

Spirit and your loved ones often come through in dreams because it's easier for them; another soul layer revealed. We're so busy during the day that we don't always have time for them. When we're at our most quiet and peaceful it's easiest for us to connect with their energy, which is also quiet and peaceful. Calm creates harmony between the living and Spirit.

If you want your loved ones to appear, ask them to show you a sign that they're with you. Be specific about your intention. They will hear you and confirm that they heard you by coming to you in your dream state. I remember my first birthday without my father. I wanted to hear from him so badly that I ached for it. I went to bed and asked him to please connect with me. Right before I woke up, he appeared in my dream. I remember feeling him and seeing him, and although he didn't say a thing, he was with me. It was so profound that I had tears rolling down my face and I didn't want to wake up because I knew my connection to him would be lost. What a beautiful start to my birthday, and what a wonderful gift from my father. It happened because I asked. So don't be afraid to request a visit, and pay attention to the signs your loved ones will give you. It will bring you such peace and you'll enjoy the experience. Dare to feel blessed. It's as simple as asking.

As our energy ramps up with the coming illumination, it will become even easier to connect with Spirit. It's a great idea to keep a journal by your bedside so that you can record your dreams and any evidence that shows up. It's a practice that it will help you decipher their messages since Spirit often talks in "code." Reread what you wrote down the night before and see how it plays out during your day. Dreams are important, so use them as a communication tool.

Peace in your heart

The most important thing when using your intuition is to have peace in your whole being. If you have this, you will attract all goodness towards you. If you choose chaos, you will have a kinetic life. Like always attracts like; another soul layer revealed.

In order to be filled with peace, you have to ask for it. Envision it in your life, your family's life, and your world. Give the gift of peace to YOURSELF this year. It's really not difficult. Just shift your consciousness. The benefits will outweigh the negatives because there ARE no negatives to this thought process. When you have grouchy people in your life, (like me with my teenagers) ask them "Where's your peace?" It stops them right in their tracks. It makes them pause, and shift into the positive. Basically, your WHOLE self can't function without peace. Raise your hand and show yourself the seventies peace sign! We're all visual learners, so doing this will remind you that you really can move through your daily life from a place of peace.

Shift into believing in the betterment of what the coming years can bring you. Think about, breathe in, and focus on peace, and you, your family, and your world will have it.

There's a universal prayer that's recited in many languages and religions around the world; the Prayer of St Francis of Assisi. The prayer's words are profound. They can imprint the message of peace that you're trying to attain onto your spirit.

This prayer would be very useful during your daily meditation, as it fills you with tranquility and goodness for your day.

Prayer of St Francis of Assisi

Lord, make me an instrument of your peace.

Where there is hatred, let me sow love;

Where there is injury, pardon;

Where there is doubt, faith;

Where there is despair, hope;

Where there is darkness, light;

And where there is sadness, joy.

O Divine Master, grant that I may not so much seek

To be consoled as to console;

To be understood as to understand;

To be loved as to love.

For it is in giving that we receive;

It is in pardoning that we are pardoned;

And it is in dying that we are born to eternal life.

Amen

The Good Life

You *do* have a good life. Sure, there are challenges, but always remember that *you* were born with a basic goodness. Some life choices can bring us some not so good results, but that isn't the whole of your Spirit, and God reminds you of this every day. We've never seen a flower, a new baby, a puppy, or a young child, that we wouldn't think of as good. If you can't agree, then you have a lot of work to do on yourself, because Spirit would tell you that you're thought process is pretty warped. You were born worthy and with a perfect soul. It's time to believe it and make the shift for the betterment of humanity. When you think you're good you do good things, and good things latch onto you. SO THINK GOOD; this is another soul layer revealed. The message from God is clear. Live a good life and you'll reward yourself and others with increased fortitude, prosperity, truth, and happiness. The Spirit of God is always in the peace and love vibration, and wants you as part of its team. The good life is NOW, not yesterday or tomorrow. You have to live in the present to find it. Your level of illumination is shown in direct relation to how you act, and will speak to the truth of who you are. It's time for you to answer to yourself. In layman's terms it's quite simple; knock off the bullshit!

This whole idea reminds me of a song that was often blaring from our living room radio when I was growing up, especially on Wednesdays. That was the day when my mom could always be found dusting the house in her housecoat and slippers. Remember when there were scheduled days for cleaning? If only I was that organized today! The song is by Frank Sinatra my mothers's second love (My Dad was her first) whenever I hear the song "I've Got The World On A String" I think of spirit and how they sure understand how beautiful our gift of life truly is. Now maybe I should go do some dusting. Nah! That will wait till tomorrow when the cleaning lady comes.

I've Got the World on a String

I'm sitting on a rainbow
Got the string around my finger
What a world, what a life, I'm in love

the other side now. The love vibration we share with them never leaves us. It just grows and evolves in a different dimension.

When people leave at the same time, it's because they had a strong, common vibration here on Earth. Ask yourself; why wouldn't that connection stay together? It's like a rocket of combined energy blasting off to heaven. How powerful! How beautiful! How blessed to have a partner (or partners) in divine love, and getting to going "home" together. The synchronicity between soulmates is significant in life and continues to be significant as they cross over together in death. The transition is made easier in the company of one another.

The most vivid example of soulmates I've ever experienced was that of my friends Bob and Barbara. My husband and I met them at a mutual friend's wedding. We had an instant connection with them. We would eventually become great friends. We often dined together, and we even traveled to Florida with them to a New England Patriot's football game when I was seven months pregnant with my son Matthew.

Bob and Barbara were beautiful, inside and out. He looked like a young Paul Newman, with stunning, crystal blue eyes. Barbara had dark hair and fair skin. When she wore red lipstick she looked like a 1950's movie star. He was in landscape design, and she was the director of paralegal services for Ropes and Grey, a prominent law firm in Boston. They had never had kids, but they had each other. They both had a crazy side, and fun personalities. When you were with them, you couldn't help but notice how they lit up a room.

My very first motorcycle ride was with Bob. His black t-shirt had permanent grip marks on it by the time we were done with that experience! I prefer cars and the safe feeling of being boxed in. Their love of motorcycles and the freedom of "the ride" would bring an end to their lives.

It happened during the first Patriots weekend holiday. This is *the* holiday in Boston. The Boston Marathon is always run on the following Monday. It was a beautiful weekend, with the kind of weather that feels refreshing and gets people outside after a long winter.

Bob and Barbara were meeting a large group of bikers that Sunday. Barbara was the only woman I knew that come five o'clock on Friday afternoons, would ditch her suit so she could throw on her leathers for the weekend. They left on their ride, and once reaching their destination along with the other bikers, had enjoyed a beautiful spring day. It was in the late afternoon when responsible Barb made the fateful decision to leave, because she had to work the next morning.

She left the group and headed home to Hanson, MA. About forty minutes later word got back to the fifty plus gathering of friends that there had been a motorcycle accident. It was Bob who decided to go, on his own, to investigate. At the time of his departure, he had no idea that it was Barbara who had been in the accident. They believe that an animal crossing the road, and Barbara swerving to avoid it, may have been what had caused her to crash her bike. As Bob was driving to the scene, for some unknown reason he too swerved off the road and hit a guardrail. He never arrived at the site of his wife's accident.

When Bob and Barbara's friends didn't hear back from Bob, they too left to go investigate. As they approached the scene of the first accident, they saw Barbara's motorcycle on the back of a wrecker truck. They knew it was Barbara who had been in the accident. They quickly rushed to the hospital to try and find her. To their complete shock and disbelief, they found that both Barbara and Bob were in the emergency room. They would die within twenty minutes of one another.

They were in two separate motorcycle accidents, but with the same dynamics. They crossed over together, from a hospital emergency room, in beds next to one another.

It was one of the hardest funerals I have ever attended. I was pregnant with my youngest daughter Haley. On the memory boards set up for Bob and Barbara were pictures of them holding my son Matthew the day he was born and of our football trip together. It's one of the only receiving lines I've ever gone through that literally left me speechless. My voice simply wouldn't work. I was too overwhelmed by emotion.

Once my grief settled, I understood that these soulmates had to "do it" together. They were partners, lovers, and friends, and had relied on one another for everything. They both lived life the way they wanted to. They knew the definition of fun and they both gave life their best smiles.

When I put Matthew's stocking up each Christmas, I always think of Barb. She hand knitted it for him when he was born. I often think of her and Bob, and when I say a prayer to them I always get the same answer back; "What a ride Kel, what a ride."

Your Appointment is at 4:30 *p.m.* NOT 4:30 *a.m.*

Some readings hit home more than others. Let me tell you about Margaret. Once in a while, I do group readings. I had read for one group of people twice in as many years. Stephanie would organize a group of her friends at her home and I'd show up and read for them. Each person would take their turn, seeing me for a thirty minute reading.

At the first group reading for this bunch, I read for Paul and Margaret, separately, of course. It was pretty unique because they were both so in love, and I saw that their passion for each other was at the forefront of their marriage. It was a profound, soulmate connection, the kind that two people might find after having had difficult divorces, challenging children, illnesses, or other difficult circumstances.

I could tell through their separate readings that Margaret had turned Paul's love light on again. It was almost a giddy, teenage love that I felt from them. How cool is that? They were on the road to happiness, and had just bought a new home and were ready for their new life together to really begin. Now, fast forward eighteen months. I'm doing the second group reading for Stephanie and her friends. I once again sat down to read Paul. Right away, he said that his and his beloved's life plan had been cut short. Margaret had passed just seven months after they had married.

I told him how sorry I was for his loss, and then said "I know Margaret is ready to connect with you Paul. She woke me up this morning at 4:30 am! I told her our appointment is at 4:30 *pm* not 4:30 *am*!' " I went back to sleep for a few hours, but easily could have connected with her right then and there because she was raring to go!

Poor Paul sat in front of me, so broken with grief. Right away, Margaret told me to tell him that the last lesson of her lifetime was to find true love, and she had found that with him. She called him babe, the nickname she had given him. She started talking about her son and his care, and then started patting my face. She used gestures like this to show Paul something he would recognize, as it was something she would often do.

Her son, who is severely autistic, does not communicate verbally. When he is happy though, he rubs his face in just such a patting motion. This type of evidence (using motion) is called "expressive gestures." This sometimes happens during a reading when certain gestures can help the deceased loved one to get their point across. Do I talk in tongues? No, but evidence can be physical, like a hand gesture or an action, as well as by more verbal expressions. It's just another kind of information that is provided through me to the person receiving the reading.

Margaret was very connected to the philosophy of the Earth's energy. She was a naturalist and used herbs and ate whole foods. She never ate processed food or packaged *anything*, so it shocked me when I learned something toxic had killed her. She had died from asbestos poisoning.

I was shown that her passing was environmentally based. I saw it affecting her lungs, and that they were covered with pustules and riddled with holes. She went into the hospital to recover from pneumonia and came out diagnosed with this horrific disease.

I saw that she had gotten this from the basement where she had lived when she was younger. She grew up in an old, old farmhouse. This disease can mask itself for twenty to thirty years. Unfortunately, once it becomes active in the body, it just explodes and kills very quickly, often within months. It did just that to Margaret, but not before she was able to give a few more lessons to her friends and family.

During the reading she told me how she said her last "I love you" to each of her children, resolving any unfinished business and giving them closure. She told me about the revolving door of people who visited with her while she was ill. She even told me she was concerned about Paul mowing the lawn, as he had already broken four mowers, and that before she died she had told him not to touch the new tractor they had bought! See? Spirit still has a sense of humor! She told me about the loose ends of her affairs being tidied up, and all the comings and goings around that. She told me about the party that was thrown for her and how honored she felt. Margaret hadn't wanted a traditional funeral so instead her family had a "Live, Laugh, and Love" gathering. Four hundred people came to their home to celebrate her life. She also told me that she is spread everywhere! I knew then that she hadn't been buried. Paul told me some of her ashes were taken to Niagara Falls, and some were in a necklace that he wore. Hell, her ashes even made it all the way to California!

The most important message amid all this evidence was about the gift Margaret wanted Paul to know he had given her; the opportunity to feel in love again. They shared that gift with one another, and proved that it was never too late to have love in your life. Some people live in crummy marriages or relationships all their lives and never get a chance to feel what these two love birds felt. It may have seemed like much too brief a time for them both, but they were blessed to have experienced true spiritual love and a soulmate connection, even for a moment. I know they will meet again.

An interesting side note to this reading: During Paul's reading, I described a woman that talked with her hands. She was upset and kept saying, "Enough already. Enough already." This was due to a legal dispute within the family. I knew this was his ex-mother-in-law, but then he told me that no, his mother-in-law wasn't dead, so I just switched to other information coming in. After the reading, Paul got a message that his ex-mother-in-law had passed. She had died over the weekend and they had just found her body. Paul would not have known this at the time of our 4:30 pm reading. In fact, no one did. How's that for Spirit getting their message out there? She checked in with Paul before anyone in the family even knew she had passed!

Sandy Hook and Soulmates.

In the same way I received messages the day before 9/11, I also got psychic warnings about the Sandy Hook Elementary shootings. Paying attention to messages, even if at the time they're unclear, is important. Often it's not until after an event that they'll suddenly make sense to you.

The day before the catastrophic event at Sandy Hook, I was feeling anxious; the same kind of feeling I had before 9/11. I was being told that a massacre type situation would occur. I was seeing children and a school. The day of the shootings, I was up early with the kids.

As I was passing out lunches, I said to all of them, "Love you and be really safe in school today." They shouted back, "We will." Why had I sent them off with that request? I had never worried about their safety at school. I didn't understand it at the time, but it would become all too clear by at 1:30 that afternoon. I let Matt take the car and do the driving that day, because I was going to be at home writing, working to finish this book.

I had no television or radio on to disturb me. It wasn't until Nancy Smith, my psychic investigator friend, called to tell me the news. She asked, "Kelle did you hear?" I said, "Hear what?" I thought she was going to tell me about a case we were working on.

I flipped on the news and saw the devastation at the Sandy Hook Elementary school. I felt shocked and sickened by this senseless, horrible, violence. Nancy proceeded to tell me about her premonitions, and I shared mine. Along with being a psychic investigator, Nancy also works in photography. She owns a company that takes kids' school pictures. She told me that at 9 am, on her way to a photography session at an elementary school that morning, she had seen crows lining up on the telephone wires at the entrance to the school. In folklore tales, crows often represent death. Some say if you see one, it signifies a death coming. If you see a flock, it means many deaths at the same time. Spirit was prepping her with symbols of this tragic incident. Spirit wants us to be ready for these types of events, but it takes practice to hear, decipher, and use the guidance given. My gift could be of even more service to our world. I'm working on that, but it takes a lot of effort from both sides. Why would Spirit want to do this? The answer is simple. It's to prepare us. That is our intuition's duty.

I've given you my insight into soulmates. They are people who have an especially close connection during their lifetime on Earth, and who sometimes even die together or very soon after one another. I'm also convinced that when a group dies together, they are linked as soulmates too. This would mean that the victims of events like 9/11 or Sandy Hook are soulmates that left as a collective.

I don't believe in just the traditional definition of a soulmate. It's not always about romantic love. What I do believe is that energy can sync souls together and "mate" them as they cross over to the other side. All of these victims had to transition together to fulfill their final purpose. It was a part of their soul's path. Sometimes this is how soulmates are created.

When you hear the bio's of the casualties of these tragedies, they were, and continue to be, amazing people. The impact and imprint they leave on our world is meant to remind us of the importance of really living our lives and being joyful people. You shouldn't look at their faces and think of sadistic, destructive evil. They want you to look at their faces and think happy thoughts about them. They are at peace and want us to be too. They are now the world's angels. The people that were lucky enough to have had them in their lives here on Earth are truly and unconditionally blessed by their continued, deep affection. Please note that the love between you never dies. It continues to illuminate you from a higher dimension.

Total and complete words of healing can never be heard in any normal way, because Heaven speaks its own language. No mere mortal words can take away our pain when faced with senseless tragedy or the deaths of people we love. The healing that is given to us at these times can only come through by way of an energetic language that we hear during prayer and meditation; another layer revealed. It's a blanket of consciousness that starts the healing in your etheric body, or aura, and works its way through your physical body to eventually heal both your heart and mind. The best thing you can do for someone that's left behind to deal with their grief is to say a prayer for them. It does heal, because you are lending your energy to them (through consciousness) and that energy begins to chip away at the sorrow and pain they are experiencing. I'm still praying daily for all those families in Sandy Hook. Whenever you choose to collectively bond your energy to anyone, it all becomes renewed by the person receiving your prayers. I would love it if everyone who attended a funeral or wake would say to those who are grieving "I will help renew you and pray for you during this sad time." This would be so much more beneficial to them than just saying "I'm sorry for your loss." The soul in heaven is already being renewed. We should help the Earthly souls that are left behind find renewal too.

For some that may sound odd. But in reality, when someone dies, their soul is regenerating and continuing with a new life. What's the difference for the person left behind? Nothing; they too have to rebuild themselves. We all become someone who's a little different than we were before the death of a loved one. It can be the most difficult process we'll ever endure, but we can and must regain our balance. The love, positive energy, and prayer which we give and are given during difficult times, will renew us all, bit by bit. This is the true message of the energetic realm. Just as your God/Buddha/Universe heals you, so we also heal one another; soul layer revealed.

My work as a psychic medium is nothing new to the
world. Psychic mediums have been around forever. For
hundreds of years, all over the world, psychics have been
foretelling information about weather, births, deaths, and
the direction of the life paths of their people. Psychic
mediums, shamans, prophets, clairvoyants, witches, and
seers, have aided society in every aspect of our human
history. It's always been, and will always be, a part of
our society. Some people may think this is all new.
Nope! It dates back as far as the Egyptian and Greek
civilizations. Psychics have always served as advisors to
royalty and have helped kings, queens, and other rulers
make decisions about the future of their domains. Even
today the English Parliament, as well as the United
States, have used psychics. It's a well-known fact that
First Lady Nancy Reagan would invite a few "spiritual
advisors" to the White House now and again.

The word *psychic* according to the online Etymology
Dictionary, comes from the Greek word "psychikos"
meaning "of the soul, spirit, or mind" and also the word

"psykhe" for "soul, mind." This word is concerned not with the brain itself, but with the mind.

The Greeks and Egyptians were very intuitive when they defined the word "psychic." When a psychic reads, they do connect to all three vibrations; to the soul, the spirit, and the mind. The mind is the neurotransmitter letting information flow through the psychic to the client. It's not the magic freak show that some naysayers may think it is. It's part of the human body that functions with the ultimate of high frequency.

That frequency was often used by these civilizations to predict war, good and bad seasons for planting crops, natural disasters, and even the fates of some of its people. Oh, geez, talk about putting pressure on the psychic! Can you imagine having to give information as to whether or not to kill someone? The bottom line is that psychics were just as important as generals or judges to their courts. Today when I work on cases with private detectives or state agencies, it's not much different than what psychics did in Egypt and Greece, except I'm not sending people to the death chambers!

Psychics and mediums were well respected for the roles they played in their communities. It wasn't until Christianity and Judaism began to form and gain power that psychics and mediums started to get the shaft. Psychics were thought to have too much power at that time and were seen as threats to the church. The Catholic Church in particular perpetuated this belief, driving psychics underground. Psychics were highly regarded for their work. Their power was so valued, that to lessen their importance in the eyes of the people they were often imprisoned and banished forever from practicing. When that didn't keep people from seeking out their wisdom, they begun to be sentenced to death for what the church considered "the Devil's work." And so the hypocrisy began. It was all part of a plan to maintain the Church's control. Personally, I think it boiled down to jealousy on the part of the priests who were not "in tune" enough to give such holy messages. Psychic mediums threatened their egos, plain and simple. They then began to put fear into the members of the church by introducing all this devil/hell crap. For thousands of years before it had been a common practice and respected as a universal tool for guidance. It wouldn't be until centuries later, in the 1800's, that psychic ability would be welcomed back into society.

Believe it or not, the Bible itself is one of the best sources of literature in which psychics and mediums are referenced. I would not have liked King Saul back in the day! He banned all the witches and mediums from Israel, but in 1 Samuel 28:3-25, King Saul pays a visit to the witch (psychic) of Endor in order to communicate with the Spirit of the deceased Samuel and seek his advice on an upcoming battle. Hmm... It looks to me like Saul had a little egg on his face with that one.

Jesus was the ultimate medium in my book. Now to some that may sound terrible, but if you really think about it, all he did he did with his spirit, his soul, his mind, and his purity. Here's one example given in the Bible: Jesus acts as a medium in Matthew 17:1-9, where he is said to have shone with bright white rays and communicated with Elijah and Moses, both already deceased at the time. My interpretation is that Jesus was linking with Spirit, as all mediums do; getting messages from heaven and gathering information to share. Isn't this what a medium does during a reading? Make no mistake; by no means am I saying that I'm just like Jesus. I'm just showing you how Jesus had mediumship abilities and honored them.

I have always said that the information I get during a reading is God given and that it's through the "grace of God" that I am spiritually able to do it, by using my mind with highest intention. I wouldn't call it a miracle, as the church or bible portrays it, but I would classify it as the hidden harmony between man and heaven.

Whether or not you believe in psychic ability or just ignore the idea of it completely, it does exist and is here to stay; another soul layer revealed. I ignored my gift and work for years, but once that veil was pierced and the hidden door was opened, I was at peace with myself. I knew that my psychic ability was a part of me, just like it and your intuition is a part of you. It continues to reveal itself throughout mankind and we're luckier for it. Without it we'd be pretty desperate people. Can you imagine living your life without inner guidance or intuition, without trust in the divine? I can't. Many people may say "Let's take this one world at a time!" I say

"Poppycock!" If we combine both worlds, think of the reality we could create; one of trust and evolved humanity! When I look back fifteen, ten, or even five years ago, I see a huge difference in our society. People are using their intuition to perform better at their jobs and in their relationships. It makes me proud to see the enlightened society we're becoming. Think of yourself and how you've changed in the last fifteen years by using your instincts and psychic self. Pretty amazing isn't it? You're aware, and that's the best news I can give you.

The Bible teaches that finding your enlightened self is important. As you have learned, I call it your "psychic cup of coffee" or "daily cup of calm". It's important to meditate in order to connect with yourself and the divine energy. 1Timothy 4:15 says, "Meditate upon these things; give thy self wholly to them; that they profiting may appear to all." My interpretation of this passage is that if you're not mentally, spiritually, or physically connected to yourself, you can't be of any good to anyone else. The balance of your life is the key to your success. In Psalm 49:3 it says, "My mouth shall speak of wisdom; the meditation of my heart shall [shall be] understanding."

If we're not grounded, how many times do we forget to think before we speak? We allow horrible words to come out of our mouths, and then the fallout begins. Yep, we've all been there, and we've all had to eat crow and fess up with an "I'm sorry" or two. It humbles us and gives us some good ole' life lessons. If we would meditate in order to keep our inner strength, we would stay on top of our game and we wouldn't have these issues, would we?

Remember the story about my daughter telling me she had visions? I am reminded of this verse from the Bible, Joel 2:28: "And it shall come to pass afterward, that I will pour out my spirit on all your flesh; your sons and your daughters shall prophesy; your old men shall dream dreams and your young men shall see visions."

This definitely rings true in my household, and I'm positive it does in yours too. We've all experienced a thought, coincidence, a dream of our passed loved ones, or an intuitive flash that lead us onto a better path. Many of us have all felt the hand of divine guidance.

Keep alive in your own life the love energy I talk about that links me to the information for a reading. There are all kinds of discussions in the Bible about divine guidance working, channeling, prophesying, and speaking in tongues. In 1 Corinthians 13:1 it says: "If I speak in the tongues of men and of angels, but have not love, I am a noisy gong or clanging cymbal. And if I have prophetic powers, and understand all mysteries, and all knowledge, and if I have all faith, so as to remove mountains, but have not love, I am nothing." I actually used this verse in my marriage ceremony. I am sure many of you have as it's right up there in the "Top Ten" for marriage passages used in weddings! I work from love as a psychic medium. I never look at my work as a "special power." I see it as simply giving guidance, by being a conduit of the information that's needed most. It's up to the person I'm reading for to take the insights I share and use them for their highest and best good and to understand that it all comes down to one word; LOVE. It always does, doesn't it? We're now moving away from the persecution of the church and from having to hide our psychic gifts. In the 17th Century science began to take over and research began to prove theory. Science would have been the "IT" job if you lived back then. Men like Isaac Newton were called the natural philosophers. Can you imagine how cool it would be to name a phenomenon and have it stick forever? According to Wikipedia, clairvoyance (from French, clair meaning "clear" and voyence meaning "vision") is used to refer to the ability to get information about an object, person, location, or physical event through means other than known human senses; a form of extrasensory perception. A person said to have the ability of clairvoyance is referred to as a clairvoyant, defined as "one who sees clearly." Society was beginning to see a little more clearly how the psychic gift worked and wanted to put a scientific spin on it.

The term *Parapsychology* explores the possibility of the study of things metaphysical being accepted into the world of science. Many cultures have different names for the word "clairvoyance." For instance, in the Hindu religion, Shamans/healers were known for using their *Siddhis* to help people reach enlightenment. You will find the term *Siddhis* used in yoga as a form of meditation and a way of clearing oneself. My point here is that every culture has a name for being clairvoyant; from the ancient Greeks, to the Hindus, to the American Indians; which shows how common an experience it is. Every culture names, and has an interpretation of, the wonderful world of intuition and its uses.

Now fast forward to the 1930's, when Edgar Cayce came onto the scene. He dove into anything "New Age" that touched on spirituality. Here you had Mr. Science blending with "that other" science and satisfying everyone's curiosity, but with a factual basis. Did you know he performed over fourteen thousand documented, psychic readings and formed the nonprofit *Association for Research and Development*? He made a huge impact in the world by helping people understand what the "exploration of the psychic" means.

Today the center is located in Virginia Beach and offers classes and seminars. It contains an extensive history of psychic phenomenon, and their programs are available to all inquiring minds that want to know!

Also the 1930's, speaking forums were established. One in particular was called "The Ereano's Conference" and was in Ascona, Switzerland. Year after year, the great minds of that time would gather and give their educated opinions on mystic visions and "elementary forms," archetypes inspiring the cultural evolution of mankind. Intuition, harmony, and peace were often spoken in the same sentences. These scholars knew then what works and what everyone needed to be reminded of. There are still forums all over the world proving the goods on mysticism. As Albert Einstein once said, "The intuitive mind is a sacred gift and the rational mind is a faithful servant. We have created a society that honors the servant and has forgotten the gift."

Our old scholars and wise, distinguished educators understood intuition and its gifts. It always surprises me that I still have to explain my work even though my job is right up there with prostitution as being "the world's oldest profession"! You have to have a sense of humor in this life! Maybe next time someone asks me what I do for a living I should just say, "I'm in one of the oldest careers out there," and make them think! I'm not a prostitute, but I am a psychic! By the way, there are no "extra benefits" when I do a reading; I just give a really good reading! (If you can't laugh at yourself, who can you laugh at?) I know spirit is crackin' up right now!

Now, let's get sex off our minds and get serious! Psychics were looked to in the past, and will be looked to in the future, for solutions and redemptions. It goes hand and hand with the connection. I love it when I read for my clients and they feel good afterwards. I don't know how many times people have told me "I feel healed." Every time I do a reading, I truly look at it as a session of healing. If it brings the comfort a client needs, what possible harm can it do to humanity? It does none. Aren't we all, or shouldn't we be, in this world to help one another? A psychic gift should be used to garner the best for others; another soul layer revealed. There's no wrong as far as I'm concerned in using my gift to offer assistance. It's when people cast fear on the subject of psychic ability that its purpose changes. *"A mind that is stretched by a new experience can never go back to its old dimensions"* said one very wise man, Oliver Wendell Holmes. Unfortunately, some people need to get out of the dark ages and come back to the present. I'm only interested in illuminating the truth of what psychic medium ability is today.

Now there are many resources for people. *The Society for Psychical Research* (SPR), a nonprofit organization in the United Kingdom, has the stated purpose of understanding "events and abilities, commonly promoting and supporting important research in the area, and examine allegedly paranormal phenomena in a scientific and unbiased way."

This group was formed in 1882 by eminent thinkers such as Frederic Meyers, who was the first to use the term "telepathy." This society is a pretty tough bunch, and nothing is ever taken lightly when it comes to their research of proving the reality of Spirit in our lives. It's so popular, that other countries have started their own research societies: Australia, Austria, Canada, Denmark, France, Netherlands, Poland, Scotland, Sweden, and the United States.

The mystics and their evidence have always been around, throughout history. It will continue to be around in our future; another soul layer revealed. It has to be this way, because the psychic is in *all* of us. It's part of our

DNA, in the very makeup of who we are. Our psychic intuition is part of our conscious. It's the hidden harmony we're all allowed to use, the built in mechanism that helps makes us tick. Some of us will tick louder than others, but we're all just like a clock, using our time to go to the next year, the next milestone, the next thing; whatever "the thing" is that's soooo important! We become like the term "Tempus Fugit" (meaning "time flies"); some people listening to their psychic intuition and using it to guide them every day; some never listening, jumping into hours and days of unbalanced chaos. You'll always make better choices by using your psychic ability and intuition.

As a society we need to let go of "Tempus Fugit" a little bit, and pay more attention to "Carpe Diem," (meaning "seize the day") by using the guidance from our psychic selves. This will serve our souls much better, by quieting the chaos and allowing us to hear our divine intuition; another soul layer revealed. The more we allow psychic ability to enlighten us and to be a part of our daily lives, the better off we'll be, even if its history is right up there with one of the oldest professions.

CHAPTER 16

THE PSYCHIC POWER
IN YOU
A CHANNELED MESSAGE

The power of YOU is not to be dismissed. You are in a category above anyone who chooses not to believe in their psychic selves. You have learned and experienced psychic ability, hunches, direction, and the following of your path. It is when you have strayed from the path that you will need to use this energy most. We have given you tools to use in such situations.

The essence of grounding and connecting into oneself is the process by which to feel love. When they say "love is the answer" it is true. It's the love of self that creates abundance in life. It will not be found in the things you acquire. It will be found inside of you.

The psychic veil which leads to the psychic experience is opening and will broaden you over the coming years. You will have the desire to enlarge this part of yourself. The very essence of you is beginning to make itself known. There is no need to go backward in life. Only move forward. All the reasons you might have had to stay where you are will be let go of in order for you to now be open.

In the coming years you will see much change with Mother Earth. She is the Goddess of all. Know that without her you have nothing. Your society is getting constant reminders from her of the disharmony that you've created upon her. Earthquakes, tsunamis, and water flow pattern changes are just a few of the symptoms she is manifesting to get your attention. You must redirect the thought patterns in yourself and collectively join with the masses to be of aid to her. Do not fear this. Embrace this change, for collectively you will adjust the level of respect for the Earth. There will be a new gentleness among societies. "The hand that gives gathers" will be rewarded and will embrace everyone's soul. Hatred will fight harder to survive on this Earth plane. Those who choose to side with hate in this existence will not be given the opportunity for life.

It will be the good in you that will allow this planet to succeed. Mother Earth will grow well under the care of your loving natures and bring many together; another soul layer revealed.

Forgiveness towards others will be broadened. People who have been enemies will join hands. Preparation is needed in order for these changes to happen. The spiritual shift you are feeling now is all a part of it. As you're consciousness shifts, you may experience disturbing floods of emotion, uneasiness, and a lack of direction that may leave you feeling exhausted. This will pass.

You and your thoughts of love and honesty towards yourself, your family, your friends, your country, and the world will help heal and redirect the life force in all of you.

Use the tools that have been shown to you through these writings and know this gift of empowerment will serve you in the creation of a more beautiful future.

All is beautiful, even in death. All is new beginnings and all works in love. Love is all. Nothing more and nothing less, as your passed loved ones now know and as Spirit always knew in its guidance to everyone.

These words are indeed a gift to you. Open up the package and enjoy the surprise within it. Your new beautiful beginning has begun. Repeating these words will assist you in enjoying your gift:

"I am the one I am to be, with grace and love to society and to our Mother Earth, for her healing and protection, for the highest and best good of all."

You are the great blessing in all that you are and all that you do. There are no wrongs from you. You're securing much love, and the compassion of wholeness from this message. Please take its knowledge and feed your soul, and then give your understanding to others.

And away we go…

WRITTEN BY YOUR GUIDES,
CHANNELED THROUGH
KELLE SUTLIFF
APRIL 16, 2012

CPSIA information can be obtained at www.ICGtesting.com
Printed in the USA
BVOW05s1531260215

389261BV00009B/367/P